PHILOSOPHIES
OF
EXISTENCE

Philosophies
of
Existence

An Introduction to the Basic Thought of
Kierkegaard, Heidegger, Jaspers, Marcel, Sartre

by

JEAN WAHL

translated from the French by

F. M. LORY

LONDON
ROUTLEDGE & KEGAN PAUL

First published as Les Philosophies de L'Existence
© Jean Wahl 1959
by Librairie Armand Colin, Paris

English Edition first published 1969
by Routledge & Kegan Paul Limited
Broadway House, 68–74 Carter Lane
London E.C.4

Typography by Keith Kneebone

Printed in Great Britain
by C. Tinling & Co. Ltd., Liverpool

© F. M. Lory 1969

SBN 7100 6229 X

Contents

Contents

Foreword

THE philosophies of existence are no doubt of very ancient origin. They go back to Socrates, refusing to separate his thought from his life, Plato, refusing to separate Socrates' death from his thought, the prophets, answering the call of God, Job, calling out to God— not to mention all the philosophers whose thought and existence have been intimately united: Nietzsche, for example, or William James, Lequier, Maine de Biran, or Amiel—even Hegel or Renouvier. But the fact remains that it was only in the XIXth century that certain philosophies began calling themselves 'philosophies of existence', wishing thereby to distinguish themselves from other philosophies, if not in their origin, at least in their structure and approach.

It is with that structure, it is with the categories of the philosophy of existence that we are concerned in this book. We have attempted to show their basic articulations, their essential moments.

It is hoped that a study of these categories—in spite of the dryness at times of their nomenclature—will lead the reader to reflect on his own existence. It is hoped, too, that he will see in these philosophies neither something totally new nor the restatement of old ideas, but primarily a call to his own subjectivity and perhaps the transition towards a new mode of thought that will combine sharpened subjectivity with a deep sense of communion with others and with the world.

Part One

I

Generalities

IN approaching the philosophies of existence[1] we are faced with a certain number of difficulties. The first arises from the extreme diversity of the various philosophical positions designated by that name.

The philosophy of existence springs from the essentially religious meditations of Kierkegaard. And today when this

[1] We prefer the name, *philosophy of existence*, to the name, *existentialism*, for the reason that several of the most important philosophers that we shall discuss —Heidegger and Jaspers in particular—refuse to be called existentialists.

Heidegger in several lectures has spoken out against a doctrine he calls existentialism, and Jaspers has said that existentialism is the death of the philosophy of existence. They have done so because in existentialism they see a doctrine and they are wary of rounded doctrines.

On the other hand, there are philosophers—Sartre, Merleau-Ponty, Simone de Beauvoir—who accept the title of existentialist. Gabriel Marcel also happens to accept occasionally the name of Christian existentialist, and Messrs. Lavelle and Le Senne do not reject the word 'existentialism'.

But if we wish to refer to this philosophy as a whole, the term 'philosophy of existence' is more appropriate. Yet even that term is not wholly satisfactory, for Heidegger would no more be called a philosopher of existence than he would an existentialist. For him the philosophy of existence is mainly the philosophy of Jaspers. As for himself, he believes that the basic problem in philosophy—the one and only problem—is that of Being. And if in *Sein und Zeit* he has taken up the question of existence, it is because he believes that the approach to Being is by way of an inquiry into our own existence. Being, then, is the essential object of all philosophical investigation for Heidegger, and he has sought to be not a philosopher of existence, but a philosopher of Being. Thus we ought to speak of Heidegger neither as an existentialist nor as a philosopher of existence.

For other reasons Kierkegaard, who is the father of all these philosophies, would decline the name of philosopher of existence: he would object not to the word 'existence' but to the word 'philosopher'. He is not a philosopher, he would say; he is a religious man and has no philosophy to call 'philosophy of existence' or to oppose to other philosophies.

philosophy is mentioned people usually think of Sartre—a non-religious and even at times an anti-religious philosopher.

One of Sartre's essays is called *Existentialism is a Humanism*. Heidegger, on the other hand, has written a letter, *Letter to Beauffret*, in which he attacks the idea of humanism. And Kierkegaard was certainly not a humanist.

Here then, we have two examples of conflict on matters of fundamental importance between the doctrines of some of the so-called philosophers of existence.

The same could be said of the ideas of inwardness and secrecy. If the philosophy of Hegel is not satisfactory to Kierkegaard it is largely because Hegel ignores the element of absolute inwardness, the fact that we cannot externalize ourselves completely. And we shall have the occasion to say that the whole philosophy of existence stems from the reflections of Kierkegaard on the events of his private life, on his engagement, for example, or on the impossibility of communicating with his fiancée. But when we come to read Sartre, we are told the contrary: a man is the sum total of his acts; there is no secret inner life. On this point it is the influence of Hegel, Kierkegaard's chosen enemy, that is dominant in Sartre's thought.

Being and Nothingness ends with a condemnation of what Sartre calls the spirit of seriousness. Kierkegaard, on the other hand, tells us that the category of seriousness is one of the most basic existential categories.

Thus, there are not only diversities but very grave conflicts between the so-called philosophers of existence. Can we, in the light of all these divergencies, still maintain that there really is a body of doctrines which could be called the philosophy of existence ? Let us rather speak of an atmosphere, a climate that pervades all of them. The proof that there is such a thing as the philosophy of existence is that we can legitimately apply the term to certain philosophies and not to others. Therefore, there must be something that is common to these philosophies. That something we shall try to pursue without perhaps ever attaining it.

A second difficulty arises if we stop to consider the fact that we are trying to find the essence of the philosophy of existence which is a philosophy that rejects the idea of essence. But, as we shall see, the philosophers of existence, and in particular Heidegger, if, as we believe, he is to be classed among them, do not reject the idea of essence. We shall see how Heidegger holds that it is the essence of man that he seeks to define and how he concludes that the essence of man is his existence. And the word 'essence' comes up so to speak on every page of Heidegger's last book. This last difficulty is therefore only an apparent one.

We are faced with a more serious difficulty in that the specific character of these philosophies is liable to fade away when we treat them objectively. Is not existence for a Kierkegaard or for a Jaspers the business of the solitary individual, the affair of subjectivity? Are we not likely to transform existence by the very act of talking about it—to transform it from authentic existence into unauthentic existence? Are we not likely to level it out, to demote it to the impersonal domain of *one*, of *Everyman*, which is precisely what must be avoided? Ought we not, then, to leave existence to our solitary meditations, to our dialogue with ourselves?

But it is only by attempting to study the philosophy of existence that we shall be in a position to decide whether this danger can be avoided.

Is it possible to define the philosophies of existence? We shall see that all definitions are more or less inadequate.

For example, in an article published in an American philosophical journal, Father Culbertson defines the philosophy of existence as a reaction against absolute idealism and positivism and as a constant effort to see man in his totality. It will easily be seen that this definition is not satisfactory: it can be applied just as well to pragmatism and the so-called life philosophies as to the philosophies of existence.

Existentialism has been defined in Rome by a high religious authority as a philosophy of disaster, a pessimistic irrationalism and a religious voluntarism. But this definition includes a condemnation and a dismissal and cannot therefore be taken as an approach to the philosophies of existence.

In his essay, *Existentialism is a Humanism*, Sartre says that existentialism is a doctrine that 'renders human life possible; a doctrine, also, which affirms that all truth and all action imply both an environment and a human subjectivity'. Is it possible that Sartre himself considers this definition satisfactory? One is struck by the 'also', which is a good indication that the definition is made up of disjunct elements. As to the contention that this philosophy 'renders human life possible', we could remark that all philosophies, except those of Schopenhauer and E. Von Hartman, would claim to 'render human life possible'. And as to the statement that all truth and all action imply an environment and a human subjectivity, many an idealist philosopher would maintain it as staunchly as Sartre himself. Besides, many people would say that the philosophy of existence renders human life impossible.

That the philosophies of existence start out from subjectivity is true; this is the element of truth in Sartre's definition. But the crucial thing is the meaning that is attached to subjectivity. For in a certain sense all great philosophies—Descartes', for example, or Socrates'—may be said to start out from subjectivity.

In his excellent book on contemporary philosophies, Father Bochenski writes that, rather than propose a definition, we must try to enumerate a certain number of concepts that we consider to be the basic concepts of the philosophy of existence and set them against the background of experiences—such as anguish, nausea, etc.—which give them their initial impetus.

This is true. It can be said, to go back to one feature of Sartre's definition, that the philosophy of existence begins with subjectivity as it is experienced in certain states such as anguish.[1] These philosophies are characterized by a common climate, by a preoccupation with certain particular experiences.

Father Bochenski also remarks—and the remark is again true—that the philosophies of existence repudiate the separation between subject and object. But although the attempt to overcome the subject-object alternative is one of the important facets of these philosophies, it is not their primary aim.

[1] Anguish, however, is not a central experience in the case of Gabriel Marcel.

6

II

*The Traditions leading to
the Philosophies of Existence*

LET us, while keeping in mind Father Bochenski's remarks, take as our point of departure an observation by Emile Bréhier: the philosophies of existence combine metaphysical empiricism with man's feeling of anxiety. This is not a definition but a characterization, and characterization is all we can hope for.

The word empiricism here refers to the element of *facticity*, to use one of Heidegger's terms, to that element of fact which is irreducible to any metaphysical construction or interpretation, and which is emphasized by the philosophers of existence. This empiricism is quite different from ordinary empiricism: it is coupled with an affirmation of a sort of metaphysical contingency and is itself in a sense metaphysical.

To retrace the tradition of this empiricism, one could go back to Schelling who sought to develop, as against what he calls negative philosophies which are according to him all rational philosophies, a positive philosophy. Now, it is known that Kierkegaard had attended Schelling's lectures in Berlin and was enthused for a time by Schelling's treatment of the notion of existence in his lectures.

From Schelling we can go back to Kant. In his critique of the ontological argument, Kant insisted on the fact that existence can never be deduced from essence.

And we can go still further back, as far back as Aristotle's criticism of Platonic Ideas. When Aristotle says that the individual is the real, he could be looked upon as the progenitor of one of the traditions which culminate in the philosophy of existence, especially if it is remembered that the same philosopher who says that substance is the concrete individual also affirms that

7

the individual cannot be subsumed under genera and species. It should also be noted that Schelling makes frequent references to Aristotle.

But this is only one of the traditions of the philosophy of existence. It was seen that, according to E. Bréhier, the philosophy of existence is a metaphysical empiricism allied to man's feeling of anxiety. This means that there is another tradition we must retrace —a tradition of religious anxiety. It can be traced back to certain XIIth-century irrationalists who have had little influence on subsequent thought; it can be traced back to Saint Bernard. We could go further back to Saint Augustine, and even to certain sentiments expressed in the Old Testament. We could recall the importance Cheslov accorded to the *Book of Job*; he called him the private thinker who meditates on his own life, as against the professor of philosophy who deals with the impersonal. We could point to some of the aspects of this tradition of religious anxiety in a Pascal in the XVIIth century, in a Hamann at the end of the XVIIth century.

These two traditions, the one insisting on facticity, the other on affectivity, had already come together several times in the history of philosophy—in Pascal, in Hamann and Jacobi at the end of the XVIIIth century, a little later in Schelling. Already in these cases we can see how the junction of the category of facticity and that of affectivity or emotivity engenders the idea of existence.

A few other considerations must be added to what has already been said in order to understand the origin and the development of the philosophy of existence.

We have spoken of Kierkegaard as the father of the philosophy of existence, but we must not forget Nietzsche. It is certain that on Heidegger, on Jaspers, and even on Sartre, Nietzsche has had a very great influence.

Some of the philosophers of existence would have us also mention the influence of Hegel. But, in point of fact, we shall see Hegel primarily as the enemy against whom the philosophy of existence rose up in protest, particularly at the moment of its birth. It is nevertheless true that in the *Phenomenology of Spirit* there is an attempt to follow out the concrete development of the human mind which in some ways anticipates the philosophy of existence and may be said to be its precursor.[1]

---

[1] What Sartre and Merleau-Ponty have in mind when they speak of Hegel's influence is the fact that Hegel, especially in the *Phenomenology of Spirit*,

Traditions leading to Philosophies

Before the philosophies of existence there had developed in Germany life philosophies, on the one hand, and phenomenology on the other. It would be interesting to compare and contrast the philosophies of existence and the philosophies of life. Between these two forms of thought there are some affinities and some violent oppositions. Life philosophies, anxious above all to bridge the gaps that previous philosophical doctrines had created within reality and within the human individual, insisted upon the two ideas of unity and continuity. Life philosophies were too facile or at least appeared to be so. The philosophies of existence, on the other hand, have tended perhaps to separate too rigorously and to isolate the various elements between which life philosophies had posited an all too easy continuity.

We ought also to mention here the doctrine of personalism as developed by some followers of Scheler, and in particular by P. Landsberg and E. Mounier. Scheler, proceeding from the phenomenology of Husserl, insisted on the person as the centre of human acts. Under his influence Landsberg and Mounier make a radical distinction between the *person*, who is in communication with other persons, and the *individual*, who is not; the word 'individual' they think ought to be reserved to convey man's isolation and atomic character in contrast to his open personality.

It was in the school of Husserl that Heidegger's thought developed. It would take too long to go into the entire legacy that was handed down from Husserl to Heidegger. We should mention the idea of intentionality, which according to Heidegger, only becomes comprehensible in the light of the idea of transcendence as propounded by Heidegger.

There are no doubt profound differences between the philosophies of existence and phenomenology. Nevertheless, the idea of 'being in the world' which is essential to Heidegger's philosophy, comes from Husserl. It is true that Husserl proposed to 'bracket'

---

attempts to go into the different doctrines not in the abstract, but as they were lived, as they were embodied in the various stages of history.

The dialectic of the master and the slave, the unhappy consciousness, and a good many other passages of the *Phenomenology of Spirit* are at the origin of Sartre's and Merleau-Ponty's existentialism. Hegel's youthful tendencies are also being rehabilitated. But we must take care not to accord too much importance, at least historical, to the young Hegel, unknown for such a long time.

On the other hand, even the pre-Kierkegaardian features which have been integrated into subsequent Hegelian philosophy have been integrated in such a way that they lose their character of subjective protestation.

the world; but on the other hand, as Merleau-Ponty points out in the preface to his thesis, *The Phenomenology of Perception*, it was he that awakened us to the fact that such 'bracketing' is finally impossible, that all our ideas are embedded in what could be called a pre-predicative soil that is our being in the world. Moreover, by the application of the idea of intentionality not only to thought but also to emotions, Husserl and Scheler paved the way for the philosophies of existence.

Scheler was one of Husserl's disciples and his thought may in fact be regarded as a kind of transition between phenomenology and the philosophy of existence.

If we consider the titles of the major works of Heidegger and Sartre: *Sein und Zeit and L'Etre et le Néant*, we see that the idea of being occupies a key position in both of them. Jaspers, too, accords a central position to the idea of being. To what we have been discussing, therefore, we must add an ontological factor, which has been essential to the development of the philosophies of existence.

But the origins of the philosophies of existence are not exclusively philosophical. There has also been the personal example of some past philosophers. Kierkegaard, for example, is not simply interested in Socrates' thought; he is also interested in Socrates the man. Jaspers, again, has felt the influence of Kierkegaard and Nietzsche not only as philosophers but also as individuals.

What is more, the question may be asked whether the philosophies of existence are not a part of a vaster movement of our time: nowadays we feel just as much attached to the man as to his works, if not more so. At the end of the XIXth century the appreciation of a work of art came, more than ever before, to involve a kind of sympathy for the efforts of its creator. The admiration that we feel before the work of a Van Gogh or a Cézanne cannot be separated from the feeling that what we are contemplating is the effort of the man, that we are in the presence of the human individual at the same time as that of the artist. Subjectivity has acquired an increasing importance.

As Helmut Kuhn points out, the existentialist movement can be viewed as belonging to a more general intellectual movement not limited to philosophy. The existentialist notion of crisis is, says Kuhn, perhaps better expressed in Kakfa's novels and short stories or in Sartre's plays than in actual philosophical treatises. Nausea, to quote Kuhn again, is better described by T. S. Eliot or W. H. Auden than by Kierkegaard or Heidegger. Without committing ourselves wholly to the opinion of the author of *Encounter with Nothingness*, we can at least agree with the view that existentialist thought extends beyond the confines of philosophy.

There are a large number of philosophers, in addition to those we have mentioned, who could be classed as philosophers of existence. There is Buber, there is Berdyaev,[1] there is Cheslov, there is Unamuno. But important as they are, we shall confine ourselves to Kierkegaard, Heidegger, Jaspers, Sartre and Gabriel Marcel.

In the case of each of these philosophers there are particular influences that we have not always mentioned in our discussion of general influences. For example, Jaspers and Heidegger have been greatly influenced by Kantian thought. Jaspers has also been influenced by pantheistic and mystic thinkers—pantheists such as Bruno, mystics such as Plotinus—as well as by Spinoza and Schelling.

---

[1] I heard it said to Berdyaev that he himself was the real existentialist and heard him castigate all the others, except Gabriel Marcel. Special chapters would be needed for Berdyaev, for Cheslov and the rest.

III

The Traditions to which the Philosophies of Existence are opposed

LET us now see to what the philosophers of existence are opposed.

They are opposed, in the first place, to the classical conceptions of philosophy, as formulated by a Plato or a Spinoza or a Hegel; they are in fact opposed to the whole tradition of classical philosophy since Plato.

Platonic philosophy, as it is usually understood, is an inquiry into Ideas which are held to be immutable. Spinoza aspires to an eternal life of beatitude. The philosopher, in general, seeks some universal truth valid for all times; he aims to rise above all change; and he proceeds, or thinks at least that he does, solely with his powers of reasoning. One would have to pass in review the whole history of philosophy in order to explain what the philosophers of existence are pitting themselves against.

Philosophy was once supposed to be the study of essences. Plato's theory of Ideas, according to the philosophers of existence, was formed in the following manner: a sculptor carving a statue, or a carpenter making a table, had first to consult the Ideas in his mind; everything made by man was fashioned after an essence. This notion of the activity of the artist and the artisan served as the model for an understanding of all activity. The essential property of all essences or Ideas was changelessness. This theory was, according to Heidegger, consolidated by the idea of creation as conceived in the Middle Ages: all things had been created as by a great artist in reference to Ideas.

The philosophers of existence reject the idea of essence thus understood. As Heidegger would say: perhaps objects and tools have essences; the table and the statue we were just now talking about have such essences. But the maker of the table or the statue, namely man, has no such essence. I can ask, What is a statue? because a statue has an essence. But I cannot, as regards man, ask *what* it is; I can only ask, *Who* is it? Man, in this sense, has no essence; he has only an existence.

Here we may mention a disagreement between Heidegger and Sartre. Sartre has said: essence follows existence. Heidegger rejects this proposition, because he believes that Sartre is using the words 'existence' and 'essence' in the classical sense; he has reversed the usual word order but remains, despite this reversal, within the fold of classical thought. He has failed to grasp what Heidegger regards as an essential element of his own theory. This element involves the definition of existence which, Heidegger says, must be understood to mean 'being in the world': *ex-sistere*, 'to be outside oneself'. If it is agreed that existence is this, and not the simple empirical reality, then we shall arrive at a proposition quite different from Sartre's 'essence follows existence'—a proposition made by Heidegger himself, and which is: the essence of man is existence—the essence of man consists in 'being outside himself'.[1]

The assault on essences, on Ideas, on Plato is followed by an assault on Descartes. Descartes' statement, 'I think, therefore I am', does not, according to Kierkegaard, correspond to the reality of man's existence, for the less I think, the more I am, and vice versa.

Kierkegaard himself, it must be remembered, resorts to what he calls existential thought, that is thought which is at once in strife and in harmony with existence. But this is very different from thought as Descartes conceived it, i.e. as universal and as objective as possible.

We have mentioned the opposition to Plato and to Descartes. Both regard philosophy as a search for the changeless and the universal.

There is a moment in the course of the history of philosophy when philosophy seems to abandon the search for one of the elements which had till then constituted its essence. This is the moment when Hegel replaces the idea of permanence by that of universal movement. But Hegel retains the ideas of objectivity, necessity, universality, and totality of the classical philosophers; the only fundamental idea he dismisses is that of permanence.

[1] Heidegger, as we shall see, does not reject essence—a dynamic essence in the strongest sense of the word.

13

And it so happens that by his genius he is able to maintain side by side the idea of movement and the ideas of objectivity, necessity, universality, and to reinforce the idea of totality. The idea of movement as essence, ushered in by Nicolas of Cusa and Giordano Bruno, was by Leibniz pressed even into a rational philosophy. It was for Hegel to unite still more rigorously the ideas of movement and reason. It is by opposition to Hegel above all that Kierkegaard forms his philosophy of existence. He considers him the end of the tradition which begins with Plato and perhaps Pythagoras.

What does he reproach Hegel with? First of all, he reproaches him with having built a system, for there are, he maintains, no possible systems of existence. Kierkegaard refuses to be taken for a moment in the development of reality. According to Hegel, there is but one veritable and complete reality, and that is totality, rational totality, for all that is real is rational and all that is rational is real. This totality is the Idea. Nothing exists except by virtue of its relation to a totality and finally with the totality. Let us take for example the most fugitive of our sentiments. It exists only by virtue of being a part of a totality—the totality of my life. But my life itself only exists, Hegel would maintain, in so far as it is related to the culture I belong to, to the country I am a citizen of, to my function and my profession. I am deeply bound to the State of which I am a member, but this State in turn is only a part of a vast historical process—the unique Idea which unfolds itself in the course of this process. And we arrive at the notion of a concrete universal which comprehends all things. From the most fugitive sentiment we can advance to the universal idea, of which all other concrete universals—the works of art, for example, or people, or States—are only parts. And this universal idea exists at the time of the beginning of things and at the time of their end, since, being the unique reality, it is the eternal reality.

From a Hegelian's point of view, Kierkegaard himself would have a place in the very development of this reality. For example, the Hegelian would say of Kierkegaard that he is the moment of irony, that he embodies the reaction of romanticism to Hegelianism —a reaction bound to give way, through the play of destiny, through the irony of destiny, to a new triumph of Hegelianism. To Kierkegaard the Hegelian would say: 'You are the moment of irony, the moment of romantic reaction, the moment of subjectivity —a moment which will presently be obsolete, which has in fact been eternally obsolete.' But this is exactly what Kierkegaard refuses to accept. He is himself; he is not a moment; he is a stranger to universal development. To Hegel's quest for objectivity, to the yearning for totality, Kierkegaard opposes the idea of subjective truth. To the objective thinker, he opposes what he calls the subjective thinker—the unique one as he calls him. By dint of knowledge, he declares, we have forgotten what it means to exist. His archenemy will henceforth be the man who seeks an objective understanding of things, the man who expounds a system, the professor. For there are things which cannot be grasped by a system of knowledge.

Very early in his life, in 1834, Kierkegaard writes: 'I must live for an idea,' and a year later he emphasizes the subjective element essential to truth. What to a Christian is the height of objectivity, that is to say, the statement of dogma, begins with the first person singular, with the credo, 'A man must always live in the secrecy of his innermost chamber, his holy of holies.' 'One must seek a truth which is not universal but personal,' an idea for which one chooses to live and die. So long as one remains in this innermost chamber, one is in the sphere of certainty. 'Everything,' he writes during the same year, 'must finally be founded on a postulate, but as soon as you commit your life to it, it ceases to be a postulate.' And a year later he writes: 'Death and hell—I can make abstraction of everything, but not of myself; I cannot forget myself, not even in my sleep.'

To Hegelian thought Kierkegaard opposes passion. The danger of Hegelian thought, he maintains, is to make us lose all passion. The man who is lost in his passion has lost less than the man who has lost his passion; the romantic, lost in his passion, has lost less than the Hegelian who has lost his passion. According to the Hegelians, at least as Kierkegaard interprets them, one must never become fully absorbed by an idea; beyond a certain point, one must control his passion. But, says Kierkegaard, controlled passion is not passion at all.

Hegelianism makes the blunder of attempting to explain all things. Things must not be explained but experienced. Hence, instead of seeking a truth which is objective, universal, necessary, and total, Kierkegaard affirms that truth is subjective, particular, and partial. There can be no question of a system of existence; the two words, 'existence' and 'system', are contradictory. If we opt for existence, we must abandon the idea of a system such as Hegel's. All that thought can ever attain to is past existence or possible existence; but past existence and possible existence are radically different from real existence.

If we know so preciously little about Socrates it is precisely because Socrates was a genuine individual, an 'existent'. Our lack of knowledge about him is proof that there was something in the person of Socrates which must necessarily elude historical science, a sort of gap in the history of philosophy bearing testimony to the fact that wherever there is existence there can be no real knowledge. Socrates defines description; he is without relation and without predicate. And yet there is more truth in Socratic ignorance than in the whole Hegelian system. To exist objectively, or rather to be in the category of the objective—that is no longer existence but a divorce from existence. Objective truth as Hegel conceives of it is the death of existence.

The opposition of Kierkegaard to Hegel extends to all matters. For instance, for Hegel the inner and the outer worlds are identical; secrets have no place in the Hegelian world-view. But Kierkegaard knows that there are within him things which cannot be brought into the open, which cannot be expressed.

Moreover, the feeling of guilt will, according to Kierkegaard, make us leave behind all philosophical categories in order to enter the realm of religious life. The Hegelian philosopher will, no doubt, reply that he also arrives at religion, and even at what he calls the absolute religion, which is identical with philosophy at its apex. But here again Hegel and Kierkegaard are in opposition to each other. For Hegel sees in Christ the symbol of humanity in general, of reason itself: Christianity is the absolute religion, because it affords the most valid expression of the identification of an individual with humanity as a whole. Kierkegaard, on the other hand, sees in Christ not the symbol of anything at all, but a particular individual, and it is this particular individual that is infinite and absolute. Hegel's system is a system of universal mediation, but there is something which cannot be mediated. This is the absolute, the Christian absolute, the Christian God for Kierkegaard, and on the other hand, the individual in so far as he too is an absolute. At truly religious moments, we perceive a relationship between these two absolutes, God and the individual, but this relationship is wholly different from those which Hegelianism might conceive by mediation.

Thus there is a great difference between the mediator in the Christian sense and Hegelian mediation.

Traditions to which Philosophies are opposed

Let us now return to the idea of a system. We said that the idea of a system is unsatisfactory to the impassioned and unyielding Kierkegaardian thought. Kierkegaard can even take the offensive and show that systems are in reality impossible. Not only are there no systems of existence, but the very creation of a system is impossible. For how would it be begun? And this, in fact, is one of the problems that Hegel himself had faced: how do you begin a system? Furthermore, Hegel's system is not, properly speaking, ever finished, for it would only be finished if Hegel were to give us an ethics, which he does not. And not only is it impossible to begin and to finish a system, but between the inconceivable beginning and the inconceivable ending there can be nothing, for the middle is to be supplied by the idea of mediation which cannot give us access to reality.

But what is there behind Hegel's system? An individual striving to construct a system. Behind the system, there is Hegel, Hegel the man, an individual who, by his very existence, by his very yearning for a system, gives the lie to his whole system.

Kierkegaard looks upon his assault on Hegel as an assault on all philosophy. Hegel is the symbol of all philosophy, especially as Hegelian philosophy was the dominant philosophy of the time, dominant even within the Lutheran Church to which Kierkegaard belonged.

This critical and negative aspect of Kierkegaard's doctrine can also be seen in a variety of forms in the works of the other philosophers of existence, and notably in the work of Jaspers.

The first volume of the book in which Jaspers sets forth his philosophy is called *Weltorientierung*, 'orientation in the world', and it constitutes an examination and a critique of science. It is not especially, then, a critique of Hegelianism. Nevertheless, there is in this volume a critique of Hegelianism. For according to Jaspers, there are two important philosophical theories which have attempted to take the sciences as foundation for a world view, positivism on the one hand, and idealism on the other. Both of these philosophies result in a negation of individuality, in other words, of existence. They disregard existence because they wish to reduce everything to what we are capable of comprehending. There is, in the world view these philosophers offer us, no longer a place for decisions, just as for Kierkegaard there was no place for decisions within the Hegelian system.

But let us look more closely into Jaspers' critique of science.

17

Science, he argues, cannot give us a comprehensive and true view of the world, for there is not one unique science but many sciences, each with its own particular postulates. Every science is founded on postulates and these postulates always vary from one science to another. In this connection, we may compare Jaspers' critique of the sciences to Plato's critique of particular sciences in the sixth and seventh books of the *Republic*. Plato, like Jaspers criticizes each particular science, on the one hand, for being founded on hypotheses which it does not demonstrate, and on the other hand, for being by these very hypotheses cut off from the other sciences. Each class of objects dealt with by the different sciences has in fact specific characteristics of its own. The sciences dealing with life, Jaspers argues, can in no way be reduced to the sciences dealing with matter, nor the sciences dealing with mind to the sciences dealing with life. Moreover, in order to grasp the essence of science, it is necessary to turn our attention to the creator of science, to the concrete, existing individual, and to ask ourselves, as Husserl did for example, what need in him the creation of science is meant to satisfy.

A somewhat similar line of thought is expressed by Gabriel Marcel when he says that there can be no comprehensive world system. Gabriel Marcel began his philosophical meditations with a study of the neo-Hegelian philosophers, Bradley and Bosanquet. Hegelian philosophy was dominated by the idea of absolute knowledge. But, according to Marcel, there can be no absolute knowledge of the real, nor of ourselves, for that matter. What do we know of ourselves? We are beyond truth and falsehood, we cannot be qualified, writes Marcel in the *Journal Metaphysique*. We constitute the domain of the non-qualifiable. All qualification about us—wise, good, bad, etc.—is insufficient qualification. We possess no truth about ourselves. Nor do we possess, as it was seen a moment ago, any all-embracing truth about the world.

Heidegger also criticizes the sciences, though more briefly, for being founded on presuppositions, for leaving existence out of consideration, for being based on the subject-object opposition, and for operating with a system of pure representation.

Such then, briefly put, is the negative aspect of these philosophies. We must now turn to their general evolution.[1]

[1] The following are what might be called the major dates in the history of the philosophies of existence: 1855, Kierkegaard's death; 1916, publication of Jaspers' *Philosophie der Weltanschauungen*; 1927, publication of Gabriel Marcel's *Journal Métaphysique* and Heidegger's *Sein und Zeit*; 1932, publication of Jaspers' *Philosophie*; 1943, publication of Sartre's *L'Etre et le Néant*.

IV

General Evolution of the Philosophies of Existence

THE philosophies of existence spring, as we have said, from the essentially religious meditations of Kierkegaard. Kierkegaard is the man who, through the act of sinning, sees himself standing before God. To be conscious of sin, as we shall see, is to see oneself standing before God, and for Kierkegaard, as for Luther before him, the idea of 'standing before God' is one of the fundamental categories.

The individual forms the realms of existence; God, that of transcendence. These two concepts—existence and transcendence—are among the key concepts of the philosophers of existence. What these philosophers are concerned with is existence in its relation to transcendence.

We are, here at the core of Kierkegaard's thought, faced with difficulties before which he refuses to retreat, for he believes that the highest purpose of thought is to take stock of its own difficulties without turning away from them. All our thoughts about the wholly Other must of necessity be tortuous and contradictory. The transcendent, the wholly Other—God—is that which is in a sense related to nothing whatsoever—it is the Absolute in the true and etymological sense of the word. And yet not only have I a relationship with this Absolute, but my very being as an existent individual depends upon this fervent relationship. In many passages Kierkegaard goes so far as to say that the Absolute also owes his being to this relationship with the existent individual: if I separate my thought of God from my intense yearning towards Him, the thought will shrink into nothing. Hence the basic paradox: I form a relation, an intense, fervent relation, with a thing that is absolutely without relation, and this paradox defines existence, in so far as it can be defined.

This doctrine is related to what Kierkegaard calls the doctrine of *how*. The crucial thing is not *what* I believe in—not the object of my belief—but the *way* in which I believe in that object. If I believe in an absolute way, then it is the Absolute that I believe in. God is to be found in the way in which I seek after Him. And so Kierkegaard is wont to say: though I may very well think I believe in God, it is not God that I believe in if my belief is not intense enough; and though I may think that another man believes in nothing but an idol, that idol, by the intensity of belief invested in it, can turn into the real god, for the reality of god is defined by the intensity and absoluteness of my seeking after him. It is therefore the *how* of my belief that defines the object (or rather, what others call object, for in reality it is no such thing).

Here we have the extreme subjectivistic aspect of Kierkegaard's thought. But it is perhaps just one aspect. For Kierkegaard believed that it is impossible to communicate directly with others and that, consequently, it would be idle, in bringing others to the Christian religion, to tell them simply and directly: Christianity is the true religion. Hence—and some commentators have stressed this point —we must perhaps go beyond the subjectivistic aspect of Kierkegaard's thought and look for something else. Another fact that confirms this view is Kierkegaard's insistence that we must always return to the word of God and seek a state of contemporaneousness with Christ. Consequently, the purely subjectivistic aspect of his thought is complemented by the affirmation of a reality which is independent of the believer. But the fact remains that in most of his writings what is emphasized first and foremost is the subjectivistic aspect. Subjectivity, he writes, is truth.

We would like to say a word about the way Kierkegaard's successors—particularly Heidegger and Jaspers—have generalized his thought and enlarged upon it. Out of his non-systematic, existential thought they have sought to evolve a system, and one may well ask whether their undertaking is not contrary to the essence—if that is here the word—of the philosophies of existence. Kierkegaard liked to call Hegel a great professor. The word, on his lips, spelled contempt rather than homage. Would it not be accurate to say of Heidegger and Jaspers that they are great professors? Have they not, intentionally or unintentionally, betrayed Kierkegaard's thought a little by expounding it as a system? But we shall leave these questions aside for the moment and turn our attention to what Hegel and Jaspers have brought to Kierkegaard's thought.

Kierkegaard, as we said, depicts the individual as standing utterly alone before God. Though he speaks in certain passages of what he calls the Invisible Church, the significant thing for him is the relationship between the individual and God. The crucial task is to become God's contemporary at the moment of his Incarnation on Earth. Jaspers elaborates this idea in two ways, with the result that the individual is no longer seen as absolutely isolated. First, there is what Jaspers calls *Geschichtlichkeit*—a profound historicity. Jaspers and Heidegger make a distinction between *Historie*, that is, history in the ordinary sense of the word, the sequence of events, and *Geschichtlichkeit* which is our particular, deep-rooted situation in history, the fact that we are born at a particular moment in the historical process. Thus the tie between the individual and previous generations which was broken by Kierkegaard is re-established by Jaspers. We are given historical perspective; we occupy a certain point in the sequence of events. Jaspers, it was seen, regards it as essential to his own philosophy that he comes after Nietzsche and Kierkegaard. To understand his philosophy, it is necessary to take into account this 'after Kierkegaard' and 'after Nietzsche' dimension.

Secondly, we *can*, according to Jaspers, communicate with others. The idea of communication had been a problem for Kierkegaard. Communication with other individuals had to take a detour in the form of communication with God. Only indirect communication was possible. And even communication with God was often indirect and, in a sense, abortive. The very story of God on Earth, culminating in the Crucifixion, is an example of a colossal misunderstanding. Kierkegaard's whole thought, it seems, was governed by the idea of misunderstanding—misunderstanding with his fiancée, misunderstanding on a more general scale between man and God, inevitable misunderstanding in the expression of belief in God before others, since such expression must take the form of indirect communication.

For Jaspers, on the other hand, communication is possible, and it is one of the characteristics of existence. Existence is essentially *Geschichtlichkeit* or profound historicity, as we saw, and it is essentially communication. But it is not easy to communicate. Communication, according to Jaspers, is at the same time a struggle;

it is a struggle of love or love in struggle—*kampfinde liebe*, to use his own phrase. Each man must remain himself and at the same time evolve with the other. Thus to the Kierkegaardian categories is added a new category which admits direct communication, but regards it as a necessary struggle.

In Heidegger the idea of community is not as central as in Jaspers. Nevertheless, we are not said to be isolated from others. Heidegger has been criticized for viewing the individual as standing in isolation. This is not true. Being with others—*Miteinander sein*—is essential to Heidegger's definition of *Dasein*. Far from locking us up inside ourselves, Heidegger tells us that we are not subjects faced with objects, that we must give up the classical concept of subject, explode it, in order to make room for the view that we are perpetually 'outside ourselves', this expression itself being rather meaningless as there is no such container-like 'we' that we are outside of.

The question remains as to what extent this 'being-with-others' is merely a condition imposed by common pursuits and to what extent it involves genuine direct communication.

There are passages in which Heidegger affirms the reality of direct communication and love.

Heidegger like Jaspers, emphasizes the idea of historicity but his own particular contribution is the idea of 'being in the world'. Thus, the individual who had been completely cut off from the world finds his place in the world once again. The *Dasein*, Heidegger affirms, is by his very essence in the world.

Here we might mention the influence of Husserl on Heidegger. Like Kierkegaard, but of course with a totally different manner of approach, Husserl had tried to probe into the nature of consciousness without reference to the world. But toward the end of his life Husserl had insisted strongly on the fact that we are in the world. On this point, then, Heidegger's philosophy does not, as one might think at first glance, run counter to Husserl's thought, but is a continuation of it.

What has been said so far does not exhaust the points of comparison and contrast between the philosophies of Heidegger and Jaspers and that of Kierkegaard. If it is true that they generalize and enlarge upon Kierkegaard's thought, it is also true that Heidegger cuts out, so at least it seems in *Sein und Zeit*, some of its basic tenets. He abolishes all that is religious and transcendent in Kierkegaard; indeed, he circumscribes Kierkegaard's whole thought by the idea of death and our essential finitude. Nevertheless, the question of God is not without relevance to Heidegger's philosophy. The idea of God, as we saw, is central to Kierkegaard's thought; it appeared at first to have no place in Heidegger's philosophy, but in his later writings—in the 'Commentaries on Holderlin' and even in the *Holzwege*—it seems that the idea of the holy is accorded a place. Heidegger and Kierkegaard are thus no longer in total disagreement on this point.

What Heidegger tries to make us feel is that Being (*Sein*) is at once present and absent, manifests and conceals itself at the same time. Once this fact has been grasped, we can inquire into the ensemble of beings (*Seiendes*). Through such an inquiry, he says, we can arrive at the idea of the holy. And once we have arrived at the idea of the holy, we can take up the question of God—a question which Heidegger has not thus far taken up directly.

The main difference between the philosophies of Jaspers and Kierkegaard lies in this: that Kierkegaard makes a choice, chooses to be a Christian, and in order to consummate his choice, comes to recognize another factor—the grace of God. Jaspers, on the other hand, merely puts before us the various possible choices, the different viewpoints that different men have had, and defines existence in terms of choice, rather than commit himself to any particular choice. Thus, whereas Kierkegaard and Nietzsche have definite viewpoints, Jaspers, influenced as he is by them, strives to put before us all the various possible viewpoints, rather than his own particular one. He speaks, for example, of what he calls the 'Law of Daytime' and on the other hand, of what he calls the 'Passions of Night'. The Law of Daytime is that which finds expression in Classicism; the Passions of Night, that which find expression in Romanticism, and particularly German Romanticism. Jaspers endeavours to show us the diverse possibilities that are co-present in the individual: hope and despair, defiance and confidence, etc. But at the same time Jaspers himself is aware that all profound thought must be limited, is profound only because it is limited. His undertaking is therefore somewhat paradoxical. He presents us with a sort of catalogue of all the possible world-views but at the same time warns us that a world-view must of necessity be limited. We are thus left with what seems to be an inextricable contradiction unless, by looking behind the philosopher, we find Jaspers the man.

But, if in order to resolve the contradiction it is necessary to make a distinction between Jaspers the philosopher and Jaspers the man, would not such a recourse throw doubt on the very concept of a philosophy of existence ?

The philosophy of Sartre has many points in common with that of Heidegger despite the fact that Sartre has criticized Heidegger in *Being and Nothingness* and Heidegger has, in his 'Letter on Humanism', elaborated some basic differences which he believes separate him from Sartre.

One might, by taking Sartre's philosophy as a terminal point, describe the evolution of the philosophies of existence as going from a purely religious thought with Kierkegaard to a non-religious and at times even an anti-religious thought with Sartre.

But it must be remembered that there exists another kind of philosophy of existence side by side with Sartre's, namely, Gabriel Marcel's. The philosophy of existence has, at least in present-day France, developed into the rival forms of Sartre's non-religious or irreligious existentialism and Gabriel Marcel's religious existentialism, known as Christian existentialism.

Gabriel Marcel was not particularly influenced by Kierkegaard, although in certain respects his position has paralleled Kierkegaard's. His chief concern is to overcome conceptual oppositions—oppositions of subject and object, thought and being, body and soul—so as to arrive at a domain that he calls the domain of *mystery* in contradistinction to the domain of *problems*. By reaching this domain we become aware, in so far as such awareness is possible, of the inexhaustible, the non-objectifiable which encompasses us and transcends us, which we have not invented but recognize, and owing to which we are able to come face to face with God.

It is too early to follow the ulterior development of the philosophies of existence, but if we turn to the work of Merleau-Ponty, we find ourselves in a position that runs counter to the beginning of our history of philosophies of existence, for here, as in Husserl's last philosophy, perception comes to occupy a central position. From a theory that isolated man from the world, with Kierkegaard, we go all the way to a theory that regards man as being essentially in the world, first with Heidegger, and in a more resolute, more rigorous fashion with Sartre and Merleau-Ponty.

Beginning with the Kierkegaardian individual who faces God in isolation, we have gone, with Jaspers, to an existence that involves communication with others and is intimately bound with the profoundly historical succession of generations and, with Heidegger, to an existence that is essentially being in the world. Jaspers has generalized and extended Kierkegaard's experience, has tried to see how much of it is universally valid (assuming that these terms are acceptable to Jaspers), and Sartre has cut existence off from transcendence as Kierkegaard conceived it, but on the other hand, Gabriel Marcel, quite independently of any direct influence, has arrived at doctrines that are in some ways identical with Kierkegaard's.

Part Two

The Categories
of the
Philosophies of Existence

IN the chapters that follow we shall try to group, in a kind of table, the basic categories of the philosophies of existence. Such a procedure will not always be wholly satisfactory; it will nevertheless help us to find our way through the principal ideas of these philosophies.

I

The First Triad:
Existence - Being - Transcendence

IT was seen that the union of *facticity* and *emotivity* begets the idea and the feeling of existence. The term 'existence', which marks the conjunction of an empirical tendency (a metaphysical empiricism, to be more exact) and an affective and romantic tendency, will be the first term of our first triad: *existence, being, transcendence.*[1] This triad will detain us longer than the ones to follow, particularly its first term, 'existence'. Once we have said all that we have to say about existence, we can discuss the other categories more rapidly. The interpretation of this first triad will lay the groundwork, so to speak, for the interpretation of the later categories.

Kierkegaard writes: 'One cannot put more emphasis on existence than I have done.' In this he was partly inspired by Schelling; he had, as we said, attended a few of Schelling's lectures in Berlin. What he sought above all was to oppose existence to essence. 'Existence,' writes Schelling, 'is that which brings to ruin everything that derives from thought.' *Tua res agitur*, he adds. And, as against 'negative philosophies', he founded his 'positive philosophy'.

But one must go further back, to Hamann, and further still, to Luther. Eventually Kierkegaard was to turn violently against Luther, nevertheless many of his ideas and feelings derive from him. 'What forms the essence of Luther's thought in his commentary on the *Epistle to the Romans* is the idea of *for me*'. It is for ourselves that we pray (*pro nobis*). Luther's great discovery was

---

[1] It is hoped that the reader will excuse the rather arbitrary and seemingly Hegelian character of this order. We consider it simply as one way of looking at the material in hand.

29

that our relation to God is not of the nature of a rational thing; it is personal and *ir*rational. Moreover, Kierkegaard puts great emphasis on the fact that belief is never sure of itself; it is forever in struggle with non-belief. (This idea is also to be found in Jaspers.) Belief, as Luther said, is an anxiety-ridden thing, forever in strife with itself. And to reach the highest spheres of belief, one must first taste the agonies of conscience; the tormented conscience is, for Luther, a necessity; the sinner alone can receive justification. In order to become conscious of 'standing before God', we must first become conscious of our sins, for only in sin do we come to find ourselves before God—by the very consciousness of the gulf that separates us from him.

As early as 1834 Kierkegaard writes: 'Christ does not teach, he acts; he *is*.' Elsewhere he tells us: 'Existence corresponds to the individual which, in the teaching of Aristotle, is something that subsists outside the sphere of concepts.' In this twofold fashion the idea that existence is not amenable to thought finds its way into Kierkegaard's philosophy.

Ought we to attempt a definition of existence? To abstain from such an attempt is regarded by Kierkegaard as a sure sign of what he calls philosophical tact. All we can do is to enumerate the characteristics of existence.

'The word existence,' writes Jaspers, 'is one of the synonyms of the word reality, but owing to Kierkegaard it has acquired a new dimension; it has come to designate what I fundamentally mean to myself . . . From its obscure origins in the works of Kierkegaard, this reality has emerged to assume a profound history.'

The word 'existence', to quote Jaspers again, is only a sign that is used to point the way, not to intellectual certitude, not to objective knowledge, but to existence *itself*, which no one can arrogate to himself or to others. And so, according to this view, neither as a philosopher, nor even as an individual existent, should a man call himself an 'existentialist' or even an 'existent', since he must perpetually doubt his own existence, since he exists more by doubting his existence than by dogmatically asserting it. We use the word existence, we talk about the reality we call existence; but existence is not a concept; it is only a sign that points the way to the realm of non-objectivity.

The philosophers of existence, beginning with Kierkegaard, chose the word *existence* over a number of other words—such as *life*, *value*, *soul*—which had previously been in philosophical use.

Kierkegaard was looking for a word that might express the acuity of the relation between the 'I' and the Transcendent. In *The Concept of Irony*, he uses the word *person*; but soon after he chooses the word *existence*. 'By dint of knowledge, we have forgotten what it means to exist. We have forgotten not only what it means to exist religiously, but what it means to exist as a man.'

The first characteristic of existence, if this can be called a characteristic, is that it is not definable, that it is not knowable objectively. As Jaspers says, we can only talk about past existence, that is to say objectified existence. But real existence we cannot objectify, nor express in words. If observed, existence vanishes.

Perhaps the first thing to note is that the existent knows himself. That is why Socrates is looked upon as the first existent; that is also why the first existential precept is: 'Know thyself'.

But the self we are called upon to know is not given to rational considerations, like the Cartesian 'I', nor to objective considerations, like the Hegelian mind, nor to the contemplation of ideas; it is indifferent to what is recognizable to all. The existent is the man Kierkegaard calls the Unique one[1] or the subjective thinker. He is constantly 'related to himself' and infinitely concerned about himself.

What does it mean to exist, for Kierkegaard? To begin with, it means to be a self-willed and impassionate individual,[2] who knows himself as such. Passion springs from our awareness of the contradiction between the finite and the infinite, from our uncertainty. Passion and will manifest themselves by the intense character of their relation with the terms that they come into contact with.

In the fourth place, existence is *becoming*. Passion and decision are movements. Existence is not definable, but by calling it a movement, a becoming, we characterize it legitimately, for we define it in terms of something that is itself undefinable. Existence is temporality, continuous becoming, a task.

It is not a becoming after the manner of the Hegelian Idea; it is not a logical becoming, but one that grows out of choices and decisions made in the heat of passion.

Moreover, this becoming may be seen to be related to the dictum

[1] *Translator's note:* This term is often translated as the 'single one'. I think the word 'unique' (which is used in the French translation) is better because it brings out the sense of being exceptional as well as being particular and concrete.

[2] Here we might recall Feuerbach's saying: 'Passion is the sole criterion of existence.'

'Know thyself'. All ethical and ethico-religious knowledge 'refer to the fact that the existent subject exists'. To be an existent is to consider oneself not as something given, but as something that must be created by oneself.

This becoming is such that it perpetually exposes us to danger. The existent is the man who is forever risking his own being. The same idea will be found in another form in Heidegger, when he says that the existent is the man who puts his own being at stake.

We have not as yet touched upon the idea of God and the religious aspect of Kierkegaard's thought in our description of existence. And, as a matter of fact, certain passages reflect the view that, for Kierkegaard, it is possible to be an existent outside Christianity: Socrates was an existent; the average Greek philosopher was more of an existent than any modern philosopher. But the fact remains that, for Kierkegaard, Christianity is a sharpening, an intensification of existence. In what respect? The will and the passion of which we spoke are in Christianity rendered more intense, because the term they come in contact with is the Absolute itself. And how do we know that it *is* the Absolute? Precisely by the intensity of our will and passion. We feel that we are standing before God. Thus the category of 'standing before God', which was central in Luther, becomes central to Kierkegaard's thought.

To attain to the presence of God, one must first become conscious of sin; to feel sinful is to feel the presence of God, and to feel the presence of God is to feel sinful. Sin, then, is the gateway to the religious life. To exist, therefore, is to be a sinner. To exist is to become conscious of the fact that existence itself is sin. But, on the other hand, existence is the highest state to which we can attain. We are here faced with a paradox; Kierkegaard's thought, it was already seen, is essentially paradoxical. Existence is at once the highest state and a sinful state. With this statement we leave behind the sphere of religion in general and enter upon the sphere of paradoxical religion—what Kierkegaard calls 'religiousness B' as opposed to 'religiousness A'. A is a state of religious immanence, while B, which is the height of religiousness, is the religion of transcendence and the absurd.

Hence, even after entering upon the religious sphere, one must still undertake a kind of spiritual journey to go from a religion that borders on philosophy—a religion similar to Plato's, for example—to the veritable religion, which is a scandal to Reason.

Such, then, is the way in which passion and will are intensified by a Christian existence. Becoming is also transformed: it is no longer of a general nature; it is henceforth a Christian becoming. Christianity is indeed not a given thing; it is a thing that must be won. One is not born a Christian, Kierkegaard says; one *becomes* a Christian; and in fact, it is easier to become a Christian if one is not born within its fold. But one never becomes a full Christian, for that is too high a determination for man. It was probably this belief that prompted Kierkegaard to say as he did often: 'I am not a Christian,' meaning: I am not worthy of calling myself a Christian. The words, 'I am a Christian', might be said to be contradictory, for a man can only advance towards Christianity; he is never fully Christian.

Thus, the ideas of *will, passion* and *becoming* are transformed by their contact—which is more than a contact—with Christianity. The same could be said for the idea of risk: for what we are now risking, and fully aware of risking, is our eternal salvation or perdition. What is now at stake in our every act is our own everlasting happiness; at every moment of our life the question of our eternal happiness or sorrow is raised once again.

The individual's thought is essentially paradoxical, because, at the moment of his accession to 'religiousness B', to profound Christianity, his thought is the reflection of the contact between a finite being and the Infinite, which he cannot comprehend. As a finite trying to grasp the Infinite, the individual himself is a paradox. But, on the other hand, the Infinite, which the individual must seek to apprehend, is also a paradox, for God who is infinite and eternal incarnated Himself at a particular point in space and a particular moment in time. That is the greatest paradox of all. And it is under the burden of this paradox that our minds toil and strain from the moment we become aware of it.

The philosophy of existence is not opposed to thought so long as it is intense and passionate. Let us recall that Kierkegaard defines existence, in so far as it can be defined, as an energy of thought. Existential thinking could even be described as *reflection*. It is not true that reflection stifles originality; it can sharpen it. Kierkegaard seeks to combine reflection and the authentic, pristine character of thought in what he calls immediate seriousness, serious youth, acquired primitivity, matured immediacy. It is true that in a spirit of opposition to the Cartesians, Kierkegaard says at times: 'The more I think, the less I am, and the more I am, the less I think.' But the fact remains that, for Kierkegaard, genuine existence is never possible without reflection on existence. These two terms—thought and existence—form an antithesis; between them there is a fight to the death. But it is precisely this fight that constitutes existence. Kierkegaard writes: 'If I think about existence, I annihilate it. But by thinking about existence, I exist. Existence is thus exercised at the same time as thought. One can neither conceive existence, nor eliminate it, nor eliminate one's thought. That is the paradox and at the same time the essence of existential thinking.

Once one has reached this stage, what is one to do? Can one return to earthly matters, to the here below? Kierkegaard thought such a return possible; by the idea of *repetition*, he sought to return to the here below after the encounter with the paradox, with the absurd, with God.

A man must choose and choose himself, choose himself as he is; he must take his destiny upon himself. This is what Kierkegaard calls matured immediation, to which divine mediation is a prerequisite. A man must choose himself, but at the same time he must, armed with his passion, his passion for the absolute, constantly try to become simpler.

This effort towards simplicity, towards unity, must be made into a lifetime task, for the simple is higher than the complex. Children have a multitude of ideas, but the true thinker, a Socrates, for example, has one idea only. To expand our knowledge, says Kierkegaard going back to a neo-Platonic notion, is very often to strip ourselves of excessive baggage.

But it must be added that Kierkegaard is at the same time quite aware that he himself is made up of dualities and diversities— infinite diversities. He is torn between his desire for unity and the numberless tendencies thronging inside him.

Existence is the palpitation of an intense life, the sharp point of subjectivity.

The subjective thinker becomes an infinite existent mind; he turns into a mystery through his profound relations with himself and with the object of his belief.

We have seen in what ways Jaspers' thought is a continuation of Kierkegaard's. For Jaspers, too, existence is a becoming; it is oriented towards possibilities, and at the same time, it is oriented towards its own fountain-head, towards its own source. This is what is meant by *Ursprung*.

Both of these ideas are Kierkegaardian in origin. The existent is that which is related to itself and to transcendence at the same time. By this proposition Jaspers explicates his own thought as well as Kierkegaard's, which is at the origin of his own. Existence, for Jaspers, is intermediate between the domain of matters susceptible of scientific study—Jaspers' *Weltorientierung* deals with this domain—and the domain of transcendence. On the threshold of transcendence existential problems come to a close; for transcendence does not admit of possibilities, while existence is essentially of the nature of possibility and at the same time a return towards its own source.[1]

We can find parallel trains of thought in Gabriel Marcel. What he seeks, as we saw, is to go beyond the polarities of subject and object, thought and being, body and soul, in order to arrive at something that, unlike conceptual truths, cannot be expressed in words. But what distinguishes Gabriel Marcel from the other philosophers of existence, except Sartre and especially Merleau-Ponty, is the importance that he attaches to the body. For the body had no place in Kierkegaard's thought, nor a very prominent one in the philosophies of Heidegger and Jaspers. It is wrong, writes Gabriel Marcel, to say I *have* a body; for I *am* my body. The body is no mere instrument, and the body-soul relation, undefinable as it is, is the key to the other relations between ourselves and external objects. We must not model our understanding of the body-soul relation on these other relations which are, on the contrary, derived from it. In his *Journal Métaphysique* Marcel reflects at length on the bond between the self and the body and on the meaning of the words: my body.

But we must not, Marcel believes, stop short at this. We must transcend ourselves and enter into communion and into union with something that envelops and transcends us—the non-objectifiable, non-exhaustible to which we have already alluded. Having become conscious of this non-objectifiable domain, Gabriel Marcel sets up a series of antitheses: on the one hand, there is objectivity, science, technology, problems; on the other hand,

---

[1] Between existence and *Dasein* there is, according to Jaspers, at once a reciprocity and an antagonism. Existence owes its being to *Dasein*, although it is higher than *Dasein*. And on the other hand, existence lends consistency and weight to *Dasein*, although the latter vanishes at the first contact of existence. Finally, it is existence that deciphers all 'codes': 'Existence comes into being in *Dasein*, becomes intelligible in consciousness in general, and reveals its content in spirit.'

there is existence, presence, the 'I' and the 'thou', being as opposed to 'having', metaphysics, faith, mystery. Problems are an affair of the intellect; I behold a problem but remain detached from it. Mystery, on the other hand, encroaches upon my very being; I am, as it were, caught in the very problem, and that is why the problem becomes a mystery. A mystery is a problem in which the investigator himself is involved.

In order to understand the meaning of existence in Heidegger, it is necessary to turn our attention to the etymology of the word. No doubt some of Kierkegaard's remarks on existence were also of an etymological derivation. He tells us, for example, that existence is separation, because to exist is to stand out from, to remain outside of. Existence is always separation and interval; existence and distance come to be well-nigh synonymous; existence is distance. That is why for Kierkegaard there can be no junction between thought and being, as in Hegel's system. That is also why sin is what gives us our first insight into existence. The first thing to remark about existence is its dissemination, its plurality. There is a multitude of existents. But the goal of each is, and ought to be, to achieve unity, simplicity. We might say that from existence *qua* extension and dissemination we go to existence *qua* tension. And the further we go, the deeper things become and the further we leave behind existence *qua* dispersion in space and time, to arrive at existence *qua* tension, and from there we can go on to existence *qua* ecstasy; there is a kind of ladder mounting from existence *qua* extension to existence *qua* tension and to existence *qua* ecstasy. Thus, existence which at first consisted in separation and fissure now turns into union. The very intensity of our experience, born of dispersion, drives us on toward unity.

But whereas Kierkegaard, in certain passages, concludes from this etymology that existence is dispersion and dissemination, Heidegger concludes from the same etymology that to exist is to stand out of oneself. This is what he means when he asserts that existence is naturally ecstatic, in the pristine sense of the word. To stand out of oneself is to be in the world. Thus, the Cartesian 'I am' is replaced by the Heideggerian 'I am in the world', for the subject never finds himself in total isolation from the world, according to Heidegger, and modern philosophy has been wrong in putting the subject on one side and everything else on the other. The subject always creates a world about himself, or to try to translate Heidegger's own term, he 'worlds' a world, for the world is not found ready-made but is worlded by the subject. Heidegger feels that a word must be coined so as to make it clear that the world *is not* after the fashion of ordinary objects or things.

Perhaps it would be useful here to show how the idea of the world, which had hardly a place in Descartes' philosophy, though one of his treatises is called *The World*, comes to occupy a position of growing importance in modern philosophies, first in Kant, and then in Heidegger. Descartes, at the beginning of his meditations, doubted the reality of the world. Husserl does likewise at the beginning of his. Kant put in doubt the concept of World, considering it an idea in which we are inclined to believe. Heidegger's contention is that we are always open to the world.

Here we might mention a comparison that Heidegger makes between his own philosophy and that of Leibniz. He says that the beings which we are have no need of doors and windows, not because, like Leibniz's monads, we are shut up in ourselves, but because we are in direct contact with the world, because we are thoroughly in the world, because we are down in the street, so to speak. Hence consciousness, to use a word that Heidegger avoids, has no need to wander out of its dwelling-place, for it has none; we are already and have always been in the world; and we have always been in immediate contact with other individuals. In what we said earlier about communication we already referred to this idea of being with others. Even at the height of his individuality, even in the depth of his solitude, the individual is not separated from others; the very notion of 'being without others' is, according to Heidegger, nothing more than a variant mode of 'being with others'. Heidegger, it was already seen, does not isolate us from others, as has been sometimes said; for him, we are by our very essence with others as we are in the world.

We could compare Sartre's views on existence to those of the philosophers we have already mentioned. According to Sartre, we do not have an essence. I will have an essence only when I am dead. Essence is something that applies to what no longer exists.

It would be interesting in this connection to confront Sartre's thought with Gabriel Marcel's and Heidegger's. For Gabriel Marcel, we do not have an intellectual essence, but we do have what he calls an affective essence, a presence of ourselves before ourselves which is a kind of veiled essence in the same sense that all values are veiled essences. And for Heidegger, it is wrong to say that I have no essence. I do have an essence: my essence is my existence, that is to say, my being in the world.

What is existence for Sartre? It is first and foremost defined by my acts and in my acts. He appropriates for himself Lequier's formula, 'faire et en faisant se faire': one is what one does. You are nothing other than your life, says a character in one of Sartre's plays. You define yourself by your acts. Sartre, then, does not subscribe to the notion of unknown genius. On this point Sartre's thought is, as we suggested earlier, much nearer to Hegel's than to Kierkegarrd's. We can never, according to Sartre, determine the true value of our affections save by the acts that define them. Our feelings are developed in and by our acts. Just as there is no genius save he who produces works of genius, so there is no possible love save that which manifests itself. Man is at first a project lived subjectively; he chooses what he will be, and he will be what he has chosen to be.

Though, as we saw, there is here a conflict between Sartre and Kierkegaard, they are nevertheless agreed that we are essentially making a choice—a choice by which, according to Sartre, we commit not only ourselves but others as well.

We come now to our second idea, the idea of *Being*. Existence is essentially drawn towards Being. We emphasized the subjective side of Kierkegaard's thought. But for him there can be no subjectivity except in relation to a being that transcends us.

In 1854 Kierkegaard writes in his journal:

'The existence of a Christian is in contact with Being.' Jesus is first and foremost Being rather than thought.

Kant had shown that Being is not demonstrable since it is position, and Schelling had gone on from there to develop his philosophy of existence. In discussing one of the major traditions from which the philosophies of existence derive, we emphasized the affirmation of the irreducibility of Being and identified it with what Heidegger and Sartre after him call *facticity*. Being is a starting-point and can never be a terminal-point of thought. In vain do abstract thinkers attempt to demonstrate Being by thought; they only succeed in demonstrating one thing: that they are abstract thinkers. The minute I begin to talk about Being, I no longer talk about Being, but about essence.

The idea of Being presents itself in Kierkegaard in the form of the 'Wholly Other' which we cannot think, but which, at the same time we cannot not think. Our thoughts ramble about the Wholly

Other like a butterfly about a lamp. We cannot keep clear of it, and it consumes us.

Thus, from the moment of their inception the philosophies of existence involve an affirmation in ontology.

We said earlier that the philosophies of existence combine an affirmation of existence proper and the affirmation that existence thinks Being; that existentialism and ontology are thus united; that there is a union of the existential and the ontological.

We already noted this union in Kierkegaard when he says that our mind rambles about the thought of Being which it cannot fully grasp, but which at the same time it cannot leave alone. The philosophy of Jaspers, too, is concerned with the problem of Being, and Heidegger writes that the only philosophical problem is that of Being.

The idea of Being is presented to us in these philosophies as posited, as undemonstrable. Gabriel Marcel, for instance, tells us that Being is above all the *irreducible*, that we cannot arrive at Being but must necessarily take it as our point of departure.

A second characteristic which we have noted as regards Being in these philosophies is that, in most of them, the idea of Being is not uniform. It is no doubt true that in Kierkegaard and Gabriel Marcel we do not find any preoccupation with the distinction between the different modes in which Being manifests itself. But if we turn to Jaspers, Heidegger and Sartre, we see that they are concerned with noting the different modes in which Being presents itself to us.

Take Jaspers, for example. From a formal point of view, he elaborates three forms of Being: Being as object, Being as subject, and Being in itself. From the point of view of the contents of these forms, he distinguishes what he calls *Dasein*, that is to say a particular and determinate Being. But to be exact, this particular and determinate Being is never wholly particular and determinate. It is forever in pursuit of goals; it is tied to a body that is itself coherent only in the light of life taken as a whole. Nevertheless, *Dasein* is an incipient particular and determinate Being. Secondly, there is what Jaspers calls Being of consciousness in general, that is to say Being as the object of intellectual inquiry, especially in the sciences and rational philosophies. The whole domain of science and analytic philosophy is to be subsumed under the heading of consciousness in general. Thirdly, there is existence which is reducible neither to particular and determinate Being nor to the

Being of consciousness in general. Now, each one of us combines in himself these three forms of Being. We feel them co-existing, and together they constitute the Being that we are. They are in a certain way united and at the same time they are at war with one another. To become conscious of existence we must wage a kind of war against *Dasein*, i.e. particular and determinate Being, and against consciousness in general as it manifests itself in science. These, then, are the three kinds of Being that we are. But we would not *be*, were there nothing other than ourselves, says Jaspers echoing one of the lessons he has learned from phenomenology. We exist and *are* only by virtue of the fact that there is something other than ourselves. There is the world and there is transcendence. We cannot *be* if the world *is* not. (On this point the positions of Jaspers and Heidegger are identical.) And we cannot *be* if transcendence which we seek after *is* not.

Thus, there are according to Jaspers five forms of Being, three human and two non-human. And the three human forms cannot *be* without the two non-human forms.

Jaspers does not arrive at a single, unified idea of Being; he leaves us with a plurality of Beings. This is in a sense a failure of ontology. The philosophy of Jaspers might be described both as an ontology of failure and a failure of ontology. Ontology is indispensable and yet it is doomed to failure. For to set up ontologies is the very reverse of setting up *an* ontology. An aggregate of ontologies is the very opposite of ontology.

It may, however, be added that Jaspers believes that this very failure will reveal transcendence to us, that by its failure ontology will reveal Being to us, that in a sense the failure of ontology and ontology are identical.

If we now consider the rôle of the idea of Being in Heidegger's philosophy, we see that he begins with the fact that we have some idea of Being, a native understanding of Being—what he calls *Seinsverständnis*. And it is precisely because our Being has such an insight into the idea of Being that knowledge becomes possible. The idea of Being is a prerequisite to all knowledge.

Seinsverständnis is not a purely intellectual understanding. The idea of Being, according to Heidegger, is exposed to doubts and to risks, so to speak, in all our actions. In philosophical reflection, which is of the very essence of man, we engage our Being, we risk our Being. What is at stake in all our activities is our Being and thereby Being itself, for without us, Heidegger seems to think,

Being itself cannot be. In a certain sense, *Sein* cannot be without *Dasein*, just as, conversely, *Dasein* cannot be without *Sein*.

Thus, on the one hand, we have a native understanding of Being without which we would be lost, and on the other hand, we are put in danger by this idea of Being which we harbour in all our reflections and actions.

According to Heidegger, it is only because man exists that there can be an ontology, and this raises the whole question of realism vs. idealism. Heidegger may in one sense be regarded as a realist, for he holds that there are beings (*Seiendes*) which are independent of us. Whether we have seen the stars or not, the stars considered as beings (*Seiendes*) are. And yet if man did not exist there would be no Being (*Sein*).[1] Thus the 'ontic' is independent of man, but the ontological is not, and the 'ontic' depends for its being on the ontological; for these beings (*Seiendes*) can be so conceived only because there is a being, i.e. man, that thinks Being (*Sein*). *Seiendes* and *Sein* are therefore interdependent.

The authentic existent is precisely the man who is aware of what Heidegger calls the onto-ontological distinction, that is, the distinction between Being and particular beings. These two concepts must always be distinguished and at the same time conjoined, and the main problem of philosophy is the quest for Being. Philosophy's unique question, says Heidegger, echoing a passage of Aristotle that he likes to quote, is the question of Being. And that question is to be couched in these terms: what do we mean when we say that Being is the Being of beings?

How is the problem of Being to be approached, according to Heidegger? We must distinguish two periods in Heidegger's thought—the period in which he produced his basic work, *Sein und Zeit*, and the more recent period as represented by his book, *Holzwege*.

What he says in *Sein und Zeit*, and this he could still maintain, is that we cannot approach the problem of Being without a knowledge of our own being. We must therefore inquire first into the Being of our own being. And the whole of *Sein und Zeit* is a study of the Being of our own being, arriving at the conclusions that we are essentially care, that care is an attendant state of temporality and that therefore we are essentially temporality.

1 *Translator's note:* In keeping with English translations of Heidegger, the word *Being* corresponds to the German *Sein* (and the French *être*), and the word *being*, to the German *Seiendes* (and the French *étant*).

What does Heidegger mean when he states that we are care? He means that we are forever reaching out toward the future, forever looking beyond the present, but at the same time conditioned by our whole past. We are in a certain situation, the present, which is nothing but a junction of our future preoccupations and past conditionings. (We shall come back to this proposition later.)

To say this is to say that care implies time. Inquiring into the nature of the Being of our being, Heidegger finds care and, underlying care, time. And he concludes not that Being is time, but that time is the horizon which must be reached before the question of Being can be asked.

He does not conclude that Being and time are identical. For he regards our being as only one form of being, and we shall find him facing the same problem that Jaspers had faced: the problem of the plurality of beings.

There is, to begin with, *Dasein*, which is not defined by Heidegger as particular and determinate being, as it is by Jaspers. *Dasein* in Heidegger's usage stands for our own being, for existence. There is therefore a fundamental difference between Heidegger's use of the word *Dasein* and Jaspers' use.

In addition to *Dasein* or human existence there are other forms of being. There are the things that we see, what Heidegger terms *Vorhanden*, such things as mountains, clouds, rivers, etc. There is *Zuhanden*, that is tools, instruments. There are living beings. There are mathematical entities that may be said to subsist, but not to be, properly speaking. There are, then, other than ourselves, four forms of being and each would seem to imply a different kind of Being. The question may be asked as to whether these other forms are reducible to *Dasein*, to ourselves. Here again Heidegger is faced with the idealism-realism issue which, to tell the truth, he does not resolve. He believes that we should be able to get round the question altogether, that the terms 'idealism' and 'realism' do not correspond to the reality of our situation, and that consequently we should go beyond them. His ambition is undoubtedly sound, but the reader is usually left with the impression that in such and such a passage Heidegger is committed to idealism, in such and such other to realism, and that he does not get round the problem as he would like to.

Let us, to get a clearer idea of Heidegger's different forms of being, look at the relation between them.

First, there is, among these different forms, one which can be reduced to another. The *Vorhanden,* the spectacle world, is only a subsidiary form of being. Initially, what we have is a world of obstacles and tools; only gradually do we come to set up a world of pure spectacle. The setting up of this world was the achievement of the XVIth and XVIIth centuries. At the outset, then, there is only a world of obstacles and tools, and to advance from this world to that of spectacle, it is necessary to abstract something from the world of obstacles and tools. It is necessary to turn them into objects of pure contemplation.

But it is not clear whether the form of tools, the *Zuhanden,* can in turn be reduced to *Dasein,* nor whether the other forms of being, about which Heidegger has little to say, can also be so reduced.

Heidegger regards the subsistence of mathematical entities in all likelihood as a derivative form of the world of obstacles and tools, although it is necessary to resort to *a priori* reasoning in order to see this.

But there remains the world of living beings. Partly in reaction against the philosophies of life which preceded the advent of the philosophies of existence, Heidegger contends that the concept of life is not one to prove useful in resolving philosophical problems. There is little that we can say as regards life. This of all the concepts at our disposal is the one which confronts us with the greatest number of difficulties. We are not as yet prepared to bring a satisfactory solution to the problem of life.

Were the solution on hand, there would still remain the question as to whether the essence of life is care, like the essence of our being, of *Dasein.* But Heidegger does not reach this stage of the problem.

Such seems to be the position of Heidegger at the end of *Sein und Zeit.* He points to the horizon that must be reached before the question of Being can be asked; he does not bring an answer to that question, for all we have discovered in *Sein und Zeit* is that the Being of our own being is care; but as yet we do not know whether we can assume that the Being of our own being and the Being of other beings are one.

In *Holzwege* Heidegger appears to approach the problem from a somewhat different angle. Nevertheless, what he says in *Holzwege* is not unrelated to what he had said previously. He has always maintained that philosophy's unique problem is the problem of Being, but his later position is that we cannot resolve this problem, because our approach to Being is in a sense an impossible one:

Being reveals itself to us by its absence, as it were. Being is at once presence and absence; it manifests itself but never completely, and we might go so far as to say that it conceals itself. That is why we can offer no possible solution to the problem of Being; we can only ask questions about it. Philosophy's task is rather to grasp the problem than to bring a solution to it. And as for contemporary man, his distinguishing characteristic lies in the fact that he is able to appreciate the presence of Being only through its absence. Moreover, we see in Being's successive manifestations such as presence, as representation, as will to power, the deeply temporal aspect of the manifestations of Being.

In Sartre, too, we find difficulties of the same order, due, as in the cases of Jaspers and Heidegger, to the lack of unity in his concept of Being. He adumbrates two kinds of Being—Being-in-itself and Being-for-itself. The one is sheer plenitude, the other, absence and vacuity. The one is Being proper, if you will, the other, nothingness. Being-in-itself is static, Being-for-itself, endowed with an incessant dynamism which amounts to absence rather than to presence. But here once more we are faced with the problem of idealism vs. realism. It will easily be seen how and for what reasons Sartre is led to assert the existence of the in-itself. There are two reasons for this. First, a kind of epistemological concern to posit some reality that would be independent of knowledge. If knowledge is to be possible, there must be something which is independent of knowledge and which is the in-itself. Secondly, the observation of certain emotional states leads Sartre to conclude that we are, as it were, nostalgic for a static state, for inertia, for restful plenitude. Thus, the for-itself yearns to pass into the in-itself. Epistemologically, then, the for-itself postulates the in-itself, and psychologically, the for-itself longs to turn into the in-itself.

But if Sartre's underlying motives for setting up the for-itself and the in-itself are fairly evident, it is less clear which of the two he holds as prior to the other. If he maintained that the in-itself comes first and the for-itself is merely a sort of gap in the in-itself, he would be committing himself to realism. If, on the contrary, he gave precedence to the for-itself, he would be embracing idealism.

The point to be made here is that the concept of in-itself, motivated by a double concern, the one epistemological, the other psychological, is primarily a response to that concern, rather than the simple observation of a reality. Have not a Heraclitus, a Hegel, or a Bergson shown that nothing is static, that there is nothing but what Sartre would call for-itself? If Sartre's motives for positing the in-itself are clear, the legitimacy of his doing so is not.

But perhaps the oscillation between realism and idealism that we have noted in Sartre and in Heidegger could be justified if one allowed that the philosophy of existence is a philosophy of ambiguity because existence itself is ambiguous.

To sum up what has been said about the concept of Being: for Kierkegaard, Being is the Wholly Other round which our mind hovers as if spellbound without ever seizing it. The other philosophers of existence share the same fascination with Being and the same ineluctable failure before it, ineluctable because our experience of Being is always fragmentary: all we ever encounter are disjointed forms of Being. This disjunction was present in Jaspers. It was also present in Heidegger and Sartre. What they offer us, then, are ontologies, but they are abortive ontologies, and they are themselves well aware of this abortive character and regard it as inevitable. Possibly this is the import of Heidegger's title, *Holzwege*, which means something like 'Roads leading nowhere'. We cannot reach Being.

The philosophy of existence is characterized by an intimate union of the existential and the ontological. The ontological is in turn characterized by a two-fold feature: on the one hand, by the fact that it is undemonstrable, that it is posited and not established; on the other, by the fact that, in Heidegger, in Jaspers, and in Sartre it is multiple. On the basis of the first remark, we may say that such an ontological position is a failure from the point of view of reason; and on the basis of the second, we may add that it is a failure even from the point of view of ontology itself. For could a theory of multiple categories of Being go by the name of ontology? Is not the idea of ontology in the plural the very negation of ontology?

From the idea of failure we can pass on to the idea of *transcendence*. Our failure is a sign that there is transcendence. That existence is always attracted to Being is proof of its transcendence. Jaspers is right when he points out that the philosophies of existence do not constitute what he calls the absolutization of existence. Materialism is the absolutization of matter because it reduces everything to matter. Idealism is the absolutization of mind because it reduces everything to mind. But the philosophies of existence do not reduce everything to existence, for existence must always be defined with regard to something other than itself, with regard to transcendence.

We saw that, for Kierkegaard, subjectivity is sharpened and intensified when brought into contact with something other than itself. No doubt the subjective thinker concentrates upon his own thought; but by this very concentration he seeks to reach the Wholly Other. Subjectivity at its highest pitch points the way to objectivity. When I have reached the limits of an intense existence I come upon Being, and my relation with Being makes my existence still more intense.

Transcendence does not have the same meaning in Kierkegaard as in the various aspects of Heidegger's philosophy. And in Jaspers, as we shall see, the meaning of the word is sometimes akin to Kierkegaard's meaning and sometimes to Heidegger's.

But in order to understand the place of the idea of transcendence in the philosophies of existence, we must go back, not only to Kierkegaard, but also to Husserl and to Kant.

Husserl believes that thought is always turned towards something other than itself. And Heidegger contends that this idea of intentionality as it is found in Husserl is rooted in an idea which is deeper than the idea of intentionality and which is the idea of transcendence.

In his book on Kant, Heidegger advances the view that what Kant calls the transcendental is not really comprehensible unless it is seen as a step towards the ontological, and that Kant, appearances notwithstanding, is not a theoretician of knowledge, but a theoretician of Being.

These, then, are the historical origins of the rôle of the idea of transcendence in the philosophies of existence.

What does Jaspers mean by transcendence? Two uses of the word must be distinguished. First, there is transcendence as the domain of Being—and here we have something analogous to Kierkegaard's Wholly Other; secondly, there is the movement of transcendence that we accomplish—and here the meaning of the word is analogous to the meaning that Heidegger gives it at times and Sartre almost always. First we shall take up transcendence as the domain of Being, expounded by Jaspers in the third volume of his *Philosophy*, which bears the title of *Transcendence*.

Beyond the scientific domain and the domain of existence there is what Jaspers calls transcendence. That transcendence should lie beyond the scientific domain as Jaspers defines it, that is, as always implying some particular postulates, goes without saying. That it should lie beyond the domain of existence and how it can be beyond this domain, calls for some explanations.

The domain of existence is the domain of possibility—not intellectual possibility, but possibility as it is lived, as it manifests itself by our will to act in a certain way. Jaspers always speaks of possible existence. In science we are concerned with the domain of what is, in existence, with the domain of what is about to be, but is not as yet. We shall see in effect that the ideas of futurity, of projects, of possibility, are essential to the idea of existence. We are what we shall make of ourselves, what we are about to be, or again, what we have to be.

Hence, all existence is free existence. The ideas of existence and freedom are interrelated for Jaspers, as for Kierkegaard, and this is one of the reasons why they are against posivitism, on the one hand, and absolute idealism, on the other.

But the existent individual, in what Jaspers calls boundary situations—in the face of suffering, in the face of death, in the face of his own inner contradictions, in the face of the problem of truth and of faith—feels that there is something other than himself, other than humanity in general, and that something is transcendence.

This is particularly evident in the problems of truth and faith. The existent, says Jaspers, only exists in so far as he devotes himself entirely to a truth that he considers unique—the unique truth to which he must dedicate his life. But at the same time the existent knows quite well that other existents devote themselves to truths other than his, which they regard as unique, and that by virtue of their devotion, they, too, come to exist. Therefore, concludes Jaspers, above each man and his truth there must be something which we cannot reach, and which somehow reconciles in itself all the unique individuals and their unique truths, and all their projects and their differences. That something is transcendence.

The domain of transcendence, for Jaspers, is a domain that lies over and above possibility, choice, freedom. Choice, freedom, possibility expire in this domain, of which we can only say that it *is* and nothing more—save perhaps, says Jaspers, by resorting to tautologies, to vicious circles, to antitheses, to all manner of roundabout speech.

Thus, beyond our own selves, we discover something which is the very bedrock of our existence, but about which we can say nothing without descending into absurdity. This, for example, is what Shakespeare wants to convey when he says: 'The rest is silence'. 'The rest' is that which is utterly impervious to the mind.

Here in Jaspers, then, we find the equivalent of Kierkegaard's Wholly Other, with this difference that Jaspersian transcendence is no longer the god of revealed religion, but something unnameable, the ineffable background against which all things must be seen.

The word 'transcendence', as we said, has two meanings in Jaspers. It also designates the movement we accomplish in transcending ourselves, in soaring above ourselves.[1] The existent must accomplish a continual movement of self-transcendence, says Jaspers, going back to Nietzsche, whose influence he has felt, along with Kierkegaard's.

Such, then, is the twofold meaning of the word transcendence in Jaspers.

Heidegger also uses the word, but with a variety of meanings, applying to a variety of movements of transcendence.

The existent is in a perpetual movement of transcendence; that is why he is existent. We said that to exist, for Heidegger, is to be outside oneself, to be in the world. But we must not think of this movement as involving an 'I' or a self in which we are initially enclosed and which we transcend, for the 'I' is not enclosed in itself; it is transcendent from the outset. Here, then, we have a mode of transcendence—transcendence towards the world—which is absolutely essential to existence, which defines the very notion of existence, according to Heidegger.

That is not all. We exist insofar as we communicate with others. *Mitsein*—being with others—is essential to *Dasein*, to human existence.

Thirdly—and this is at least as important as transcendence towards the world—we are continually transcending towards the future. The place of the ideas of *future* and *possibility* in the philosophies of existence has already been emphasized.

Thus, we are always in the world, always with others, always reaching out towards the future. These are the first three meanings of the word 'transcendence' in Heidegger, and they correspond to the second meaning of the word in Jaspers. We are perpetually transcending ourselves. But the word has two more meanings in Heidegger, which are akin to Jaspers' first meaning and the classical

[1] For distinctions between the different modes of transcendence in this second sense, see my *La pensée de l'existence* (Flammarion, 1952).

meaning of the word. We transcend perpetually towards Being. We transcend towards Being in virtue of our understanding of the ontological distinction which permits us to distinguish Being from individual beings. And at the same time, we know that we exist in the sense that we stand above nothingness, that we transcend ourselves out of nothingness. It remains to be seen—and we shall come back to the problem—what nothingness is. Is it not, in the end, the same thing as Being? If so, our last two modes of transcendence would in reality be identical.

But for the moment we may say that Heidegger elaborates five modes of transcendence, of which transcendence towards Being comes nearest to the ordinary meaning of the word.

Several of these meanings of the word are to be found in Sartre, who speaks rather often of transcendence towards the world and transcendence towards the future.

In this brief discussion of the idea of transcendence, we began with Kierkegaard's Wholly Other, touched upon the two senses of the word in Jaspers, and saw the five modes of transcendence in Heidegger, of which only two resemble the classical idea of transcendence, the remaining three being, like Sartrian transcendence, what could be called 'horizontal' transcendence.

The question may be asked: have the philosophers of existence put the word 'transcendence' to proper use? Gabriel Marcel has said that it is illegitimate to use the word in the various senses that Heidegger and Sartre use it, that the word applies primarily to God in so far as he is beyond qualification. Marcel is an advocate of the classical meaning of the word.

But one may go further and ask whether Heidegger is not more faithful to the origins of the word than even the classical meaning, whether he does not hark back to a more ancient meaning of the word. The word 'transcend' suggests an upward movement and consequently one may agree with Heidegger's remark that the *Dasein* alone transcends; God, just because he is up above, could not be said to transcend. To transcend is to make a movement, and it is the *Dasein*, the human existent, that makes the movement of transcendence.

Thus, one could conclude that the philosophies of existence go back to a more ancient, more pristine sense of the word 'existence'.

II

The Second Triad:
Possibility and Project - Origin - Now,
Situation, Instant

WE have examined what we called the first three philosophical categories of existence: the concept of existence itself, the concepts of Being, and the concept of transcendence.

We would now like to study a second series of categories relating to time, after briefly discussing the rôle of the idea of time itself in the philosophies of existence. The time-categories to be studied are: first, the concepts of *possibility* and *project*; second, the concept of *origin* or *source*, especially as developed by Jaspers; third, the three concepts of *now*, *situation*, and the *instant*.

But first, let us take up the idea of time in general.

It was already seen, apropos of Kierkegaard, that existence is essentially a becoming. But, as we took care to point out, the Kierkegaardian notion of becoming, and the existential notion in general, are radically different from the Hegelian notion of becoming. For time, as Hegel sees it, is a continuous becoming, a becoming that is rational and explicable. Kierkegaardian time, on the other hand, is a discontinuous becoming, made up of crises, advancing by leaps and bounds; it is an inexplicable becoming, containing irreducibly novel elements—the upshots of our decisions. Time, for Hegel, is the becoming of the Idea. For Kierkegaard, it is the becoming of the human individual himself. Time, for Hegel, leads us to the Absolute, which will reveal itself at the end of time and is potentially present from the beginning of time; so that time leads us to an eternity which goes beyond time. For Kierkegaard, there is a centre to time: the paradoxical moment when the Eternal turned himself into man, the moment of Incarnation, a moment which cannot, properly speaking, be *thought*, and is an enigma, a mystery, a scandal.

Several contemporary schools of philosophy, and pragmatism in particular, have been described as time-philosophies. The term is also applicable to the philosophy of Bergson and to the philosophies of existence.

But, while we are on the subject of time, we ought to make some distinctions between Kierkegaard and his successors, especially Jaspers and Heidegger. To the Kierkegaardian position, which shuts the individual up, as it were, within his subjectivity and his subjective relationship with God, Jaspers and Heidegger bring the idea of what they call *Geschichtlichkeit*—the individual's deep historicity. We have already dwelt upon the difference of meaning between the words *Geschichte* and *Historie* in German. *Historie* simply denotes the chronological recording of events, but not in depth, so to speak, while *Geschichte* (historicity) is the very source of historical time—the fact that an existent individual is deeply grounded in a temporal situation, in a historical setting. Thus, to the Kierkegaardian idea of the individual, Jaspers and Heidegger add the idea of the individual's deep historicity.

What is historicity according to Jaspers? Historicity, says Jaspers, is the unity of the being that I am and existence; it is the unity of *Dasein* and existence. It is the unity of necessity and freedom. I am in effect situated at a particular point in space and in time. This is the import of the idea of *situation*, which we shall examine later. I must acknowledge and assume this situation, and it is only by doing so that I become aware of my historicity.

We can now consider our first time-category, which is that of *possibility* and *project*, and which therefore involves the idea of the future.

Indeed, the primal dimension of time, for the philosophers of existence, is the future. The individual, properly speaking, is *not*, but is *about to be*; he is a *task* that he sets himself. No doubt Hegel had already proclaimed the future as the pre-eminent dimension of time, but in Kierkegaard and his successors the proclamation takes on a different accent, for here the future is the future of the individual, a subjectively felt future.

The first dimension of time, the 'first ecstasy of time', to use Heidegger's expression, is the future.[1] We are always in the

---

[1] We must not overlook the fact that Sartre is not in agreement with Heidegger on this point. More akin to Husserl in this respect, he maintains that the primal

planning stage, in 'projection'. What Heidegger means when he speaks of the 'ecstasy of time', of the 'ec-static character of time' is that time is never enclosed within itself, that it is, so to speak, in flight before itself. Just as existence is outside itself, so time is at every instant outside itself, in flight before itself.

Now, the idea of *possibility* is central to Kierkegaard's thought. One of his main charges against Hegel is that he leaves no room in his System for genuinely lived possibility; he makes possibility impossible and thus deprives man of the oxygen necessary to his life and actions. A world that does not admit of possibility, Kierkegaard believed, is a world in which the individual suffocates. It is particularly in the *Concept of Dread* that Kierkegaard develops the idea of possibility, discovering in dread the apparition of temptational possibilities which plunge us into a state of giddiness and bewilderment. But if there are temptational possibilities, possibilities which degrade us, there are also possibilities which elevate us, which deliver us from temptation, and these are essentially *religious possibilities*, rendering possible things that to pedestrian reason would appear impossible.[1] Here we might mention a philosopher not included in our study, Cheslov, who dwells at length upon this point—the possibility of impossibility—in his definition of faith as superior to reason.

Jaspers, as it was seen, has a great deal to say about *possible existence*, meaning by this that existence is not ready-made, but always about to be. Man is always ahead of himself, says Heidegger. And from here it is but a step to Sartre's statement that the existent is a *pro-ject*. The idea of project is central to Sartre's philosophy, and central also to Heidegger's. The existent makes himself; he must above all not be tied down to his past; he must not let time fossilize, whether at some point in the past or at some point in the future. To yoke oneself to some moment of one's past, to refer continually back to some prior happening or, for that matter, to clutch in anticipation to some future event—a post, for example,

[1] It is thus seen that the idea of a duality of possibilities—possibilities that degrade us, possibilities that elevate us—is the bridge taking us from unauthenticity to authenticity in Kierkegaard.

dimension of time is the present, that it is in terms of the present, that we form the future and the past.

But it must also be noted that the present as Sartre conceives it is constantly vanishing, receding, as it were before itself, so that we may wonder how, on the basis of such an unstable foundation, the other dimensions of time are to be construed.

that one has coveted ever since youth—is to stop the flow of time indispensable to the *for-itself*, to mould oneself after a petrified past or a petrified future, which cease to belong to the *for-itself* and lapse into the *in-itself*. This leads Sartre to his analyses of self-deception (*mauvaise foi*): self-deception is a disregard of what one really is; it is an attempt to bring time to a standstill, and therefore a falsification of time.

We can now go on to our second category, to the idea of *origin* or *source*.

'Generally speaking,' writes Kierkegaard as early as 1835, 'all veritable development is a return back to our origins,' and he cites the example of great artists who 'go forward by going backwards'. In our own lives the first instants, the beginnings are of crucial importance. The genuine individual, the existent, will therefore seek to know himself by turning back towards his origin; and he will, at the same time, seek self-knowledge by turning forward towards his future. He will thus unite his past and his future in the fullness of the present.

Kierkegaard invites us to go back to what is pristine, to what is primitive, to what is primogenial. He believes that existence should recover its eternal primitivity. And as a Christian, too, Kierkegaard wants to go back to the source, back to Christ himself. We must, he says, sweep away the centuries that separate us from Christ and estrange us from him; we must become contemporaneous with Christ himself: this is the essence of the act of faith. If we succeed in this act, we shall be just as near Christ as were his disciples in Jerusalem.

In the other philosophers of existence, too, we find similar efforts to go back to the source. Thus Heidegger, no doubt in a different way and in a wholly different domain, would have us hark back to the earliest Greek philosophers. And Jaspers says that, in the study of every great philosopher, we must endeavour to discover the source of his thought (*Ursprung*). Whether we are studying Descartes, or Leibniz, or Nietzsche, or Plato, there is always a core, a fundamental intuition—of which Bergson also spoke—that must be excavated from beneath the more or less superficial, rational superstructures of the system. In a long article on Descartes, Jaspers attempts to show that there is a valid element in Cartesianism, but that it is vitiated and falsified by the systematization, by the rationalization that Descartes imposes upon it.

After the categories of *possibility* and *origin*, we come to the last category of our second triad, bearing the triple title of *now*, *situation*, and *instant*.

These three ideas are in reality radically different from one another. What Heidegger would particularly emphasize is that it is not with the present that we must begin if we wish to gain an insight into the constitution of time: we must begin with the past or with the future, for the present is nothing but the junction of the past and the future. But this junction can be effected in several ways. It can be effected superficially, and in that case what we have are *nows*, the sequence of *nows* that constitute unauthentic time. Heidegger makes certain distinctions about time. First, there is pragmatic time (though he does not refer to it by this name), the time of everyday life—what he calls time *for*. Every time we act, we do so with a practical end in view. This, for instance is the hour *for* studying philosophy. The next hour may be reserved *for* lunch, etc. Time in everyday life is always time *for*. But, on the basis of this everyday time, science has created abstract time. It is here that the idea of *now* comes in. Out of pragmatic time, which consists of blocks of duration each destined to a particular purpose, the mind makes a homogenous and infinite time. This homogenous and infinite time is posterior to everyday time and derived from it. And it is into this scientific time that *nows* are incorporated.

We must therefore make a thorough distinction between the idea of *now* and the idea of the *instant*, which we shall consider after the ideas of *facticity* and *situation*.

There is an element of fact that is neither reducible to, nor deducible from, anything else; and this element of facticity, as Heidegger and Sartre call it, is inherent to our very essence.

If we examine this element closely, we shall arrive at what Heidegger terms *Geworfenheit*, that is to say the fact that we find ourselves thrown into this world without knowing why. One may wonder whether this Heideggerian conception is at all meaningful independently of religious presuppositions; for perhaps only if there lingers in the back of our mind the notion of a deity who is to bring us aid and comfort, can we be surprised and shocked to find that we are here without aid. Thus our feeling of abandonment may simply be due to our abandonment of the notion of a benevolent deity.

But let us leave this question aside for the moment. What we wanted to emphasize in connection with *Geworfenheit*—our 'throwness' into the world—is that we are facticity through and through, so much so that even the element of freedom that we possess is characterized as facticity. Our very freedom is facticity.

We may now pass on to the idea of *situation*. No doubt every philosophy is concerned with man's situation in the universe. But only when a thinker has a quasi-affective conception of the human situation can we compare him to the philosophers of existence. Thus, man as Descartes conceives of him—placed above pure mechanism and below divine perfection—cannot, properly speaking, be said to be in a situation in the existential sense of the word. But when a thinker such as Pascal represents man as standing between two infinities, in the silence and as it were under the silence of the firmament, alone before his God, then we recognize a conception of human situation akin to that of the philosophies of existence.

The idea of *situation* has a great importance in all these philosophies. When possibility is placed in actuality it is in a situation. We have already mentioned the rôle this idea plays, implicitly at least, in Kierkegaard's thought. No philosophy was ever more motivated by a particular situation than Kierkegaard's; it was, as we saw, in response to the problems raised by his engagement and his relations to Regina, his fiancée, that he developed his entire philosophy. It is on his private situation, then, that Kierkegaard meditates. His private situation forms the cornerstone of his thought, and his thought in turn forms the cornerstone of the subsequent philosophies of existence.

But not all situations are of this kind; there are also philosophical situations. This, for example, is what Jaspers means when he says that today one cannot do philosophy as one did philosophy before those momentous events that we call Nietzsche and Kierkegaard. The philosopher's situation, therefore, is at least twofold: there is his private situation and there is his philosophical situation.

In Gabriel Marcel's thought the idea of situation is equally present and it enters into his very conception of metaphysics. Not only must we never abstract a problem from the situation in which it arises, but also the domain of metaphysics is that in which our own situation, the situation of the questioner, is called into question, becomes the object of our scrutiny; thus, it is when our situation is itself involved in the problem, when the question recoils back at the questioner, that the problem is transformed into mystery and the realm of metaphysics opens up before us.

The importance of the idea of situation in Sartre's thought is well known. All our acts, he maintains, can be interpreted differently depending on whether they are interpreted in terms of our *freedom* or in terms of our *situation*. Sartre's position here is not free of difficulties, for he affirms at the same time that our situation is dependent largely on our freedom. He regards freedom as the more basic idea, to which the idea of situation must be reduced; the situation only exists because our freedom comes up against such or such empirical facts, and these facts in turn, only exist in relation to the goals we set ourselves. Obstacles, then, are obstacles only because we set ourselves goals, and these goals, Sartre declares, are set up by our freedom.

Finally, we must mention what Jaspers calls *boundary situations*. In the face of evil, war, suffering, death, our existence is tried to the extreme, finds itself at its own extremity, realizes that it exists only because there is something else which it cannot surmount and before which it must finally assume silence: transcendence.

We come now to the idea of *instant*. This idea, too, is in a sense central to Kierkegaard's thought. We have spoken of the instant of Incarnation as the centre of history according to Kierkegaard. It is also in the instant that we can break with our conceptual habits of thought and our social habits in order to commune with that centre of profound history. Here Kierkegaard invokes both the *Parmenides* of Plato, whose third hypothesis concerns the idea of instant, and the Gospel's assertion that we transcend time in the act of receiving the good tidings.

The *instant* springs from the junction of the past and the future authentically conceived, just as the *now* springs from unauthentic past and future. But the instant lifts us above the planes of past and future; the instant, says Kierkegaard, is the encounter of time and eternity; the instant, for Heidegger, is the moment when with resolute decision we take ourselves upon ourselves and, uniting our origins and projects, accept the responsibility of what we are.

We can draw a parallel between this concept and the doctrine of Jaspers according to which what is highest in the hierarchy of realities is also the most precarious, the most fragile, revealing itself only in flashes. For a moment the flashes light up the darkness of our night; they are the carrier of all values. In a view such as this, value may be said to be inversely proportional to stability.

III

The Third Triad:
Choice and Freedom - Nothingness
and Dread - Authenticity

WE shall now take up a third triad of categories: *choice* and *freedom*; *nothingness* and *dread*; *authenticity* and *repetition*. It was seen earlier that existence is time; it will now be seen that it is choice and freedom within time. It was seen that existence is related to Being, but that it is also related to that rarefied being, that diminished being—possibility; and now the diminishing of Being will continue to the point of nothingness; situation will become situation of dread. And from *nothingness* and *dread* we shall be able to go back to the idea of *origin* which will, in the idea of *repetition*, reveal itself as *authenticity*.

The first concept we shall take up is that of choice. It will easily be seen that choice occupies a very important place in Kierke-gaard's thought. The title of one of his books is *Either/Or*. We must choose to choose. Indeed, the idea of possibility would be nugatory were it not related to the idea of choice—choice within time. Kierkegaard elaborates several levels of choice. First, there is superficial choice, belonging to what he calls the 'aesthetic stage' —the stage of pure pleasure. Then come ethical choice and religious choice.

No doubt Kierkegaard sees a beauty and a purpose to the ethical choice; some of his writings may even be read as an apology of that choice. To choose the ethical is to become part of the community, find a vocation, marry, perform some function in life. But on the other hand, Kierkegaard believes that there is something higher than all this, higher than the ethical; this belief finds its practical expression in the breaking of his engagement, its philosophical expression in *Fear and Trembling*. For there is

E   57

what Kierkegaard calls a 'suspension of the ethical', a suspension prompted by the fact that I hear the voice of God, and God can absolve us even from our moral obligations.

On this matter one could compare the philosophies—always dissimilar and yet always calling for comparison—of Nietzsche and Kierkegaard.

Thus the choice is between the aesthetic, which is a region of scarce faith and scarce choice, the ethical, which is a mature and integrating choice, and finally the religious, which is abrupt and disintegrating at first.

But how can we know that it is the voice of God we hear? How does Abraham know that it is the voice of God bidding him to go and sacrifice Isaac? No external sign can here be of any use whatsoever, and Kierkegaard lays great emphasis on this point, which was to become central to the philosophy of existence as a whole. Independently of all established values, independently of all determined essences, through our own subjectivity, we shall decide that what we hear is the voice of God.

In his lecture, *Existentialism is a Humanism*, Sartre, so unlike and in many ways so opposed as he is to Kierkegaard, advocates the same point of view.

This, Kierkegaard believes, is not a matter of objective considerations like those of the Hegelians, nor of scientific considerations like those of the Cartesian or Kantian philosophies; it is above all a matter of being oneself in one's relations with the Absolute. And even if the choice we make should involve consequences that appear foreign to the ethical, we must accept the responsibility of our choice; though there are no objective signs to point the way, we must nevertheless go beyond the ethical stage.

Thus, behind the idea of choice we discover the idea of subjectivity which, as we saw in connection with the idea of existence, occupies a very important place in Kierkegaard's thought.

The idea of choice is also present in the philosophy of Jaspers; indeed, his whole philosophy, at least as it is set forth in the second volume of his massive work, *Philosophie*, may be looked upon as a kind of catalogue of the various choices open to us.

We are here faced with a problem to which we have already alluded: is the idea of a list of choices compatible with genuine existential thought? For example, Jaspers pairs off what he calls the choice of confidence and the choice of defiance; he contrasts, as it was seen, the 'Law of Daytime' and the 'Passions of Night'.

The 'Law of Daytime' is rather similar to the ethical stage in Kierkegaard. It would have us follow the dictates of reason, find a vocation, etc.; the 'Passions of Night', the romantic 'Passions of Night' would have us fly in the face of the 'Law of Daytime'. (The opposition here is not the Kierkegaardian opposition between the ethical and the religious, for although Jaspers' 'Law of Daytime' corresponds closely to the ethical stage in Kierkegaard, the 'Passions of Night' cannot be said to correspond to Kierkegaard's religious stage.) In the 'Law of Daytime' and 'Passions of Night', then, we have conflicting attitudes, and both attitudes, Jaspers believes, can be authentic. The question is whether Jaspers, in compiling a catalogue of possible choice, remains faithful to the spirit of the philosophy of existence, to the spirit of his own philosophy; for he tells us at the same time that the way to profundity is by way of narrowness. Thus as an existent, Jaspers would choose one specific course, either the 'Law of Daytime' or the 'Passions of Night'. But as a philosopher reflecting on existence and not on any one existent, he ventures to make a list of the various possible choices. There is nevertheless a difficulty here, a sort of antinomy in Jaspers' thought. We can do one of two things: either draw up a list of possible choices or adopt and put into practice one specific choice. It would seem that both cannot be done at the same time.

But the main point we wanted to make is the importance of the idea of choice in Jaspers, its elemental character. All choice, so long as it is authentic, takes us nearer to the *origin*, leads us to the *instant*.

The idea of choice can also be found in the philosophy of Sartre. Sartre insists above all on the fact that it is by my choice that I create values. I am the unfounded foundation of all values; since I am the one who founds everything, I myself am without foundation; I am the being that brings values into the world and for that very reason I myself am unjustifiable. Sartre, like Kierkegaard, insists that there are no external signs to guide me; I must make my own rules and make them alone: 'There was in his world,' Sartre writes in *The Age of Reason*, 'no evil or good save what he set up as such. All round him things had formed a circle and waited without making a sign; he stood alone in the midst of a monstrous silence, alone and free, without recourse or excuse, irrevocably condemned, condemned to be free.'

From here we can pass on to the idea of freedom. It is the question of freedom that brings Kierkegaard into conflict with

Hegel. Freedom, says Kierkegaard, is man's greatness and grandeur. His charge against Hegel is that he has left no room in his system for our feeling of freedom.

The idea of freedom is also to be found at the centre of Jaspers' thought. How is it, he asks, that we are free, how is it that existence is essentially freedom? It is because transcendence is concealed from us. If transcendence were revealed to us directly, we should not, says Jaspers, be able to be free: transcendence would dominate us. Transcendence conceals or veils itself. Transcendence, to use a Kierkegaardian expression taken over by Jaspers, refrains from revealing itself save indirectly so as to put our freedom to the test. Accordingly, the domain of existence is the domain of freedom, and hence that of possibility, project and choice.

The same is true of Sartre; indeed, it may be said that Sartre's whole thought revolves round the idea of freedom.

Freedom, says Sartre, is the sole foundation of values. It is true that he lays down a sort of *in actu* universalization of values: my freedom is interdependent with that of all others; nevertheless, my freedom is basically *my* freedom. No other can nor has to follow the path that I follow. Akin to the Kafka character for whom opens a door which can open for no other, the existent knows that his problem is his alone, and his solution only his.

Here one could underscore the meeting in Sartre of two traditions both going back to Kant, one via Lagneau and Alain and the other via Heidegger.

The Sartrian doctrine of freedom has a number of peculiar features. To begin with, Sartre maintains that if a being is free, he is always free, in all situations, under all circumstances. In classical theories of freedom we are said to be free at certain moments and not free at certain others. But Sartre tells us that if man is free, he is always free. It would be incomprehensible, he argues, that freedom should disappear and then reappear at some later moment. Consequently we are equally free whether we decide to be cowardly or courageous. Whichever way we act, our responsibility is in no way cut down, on the contrary, since in either case there is a choice: in both cases there is decision and freedom.

The view that man is equally free at all times is one which had not been previously maintained; it is to Sartre's credit to have put forward this view which, though tending to destroy the very feeling of freedom that Sartre means to safeguard, offers us a new subject for reflection.

What is more, freedom always appears in Sartre—and this could also be said of Jaspers and Heidegger—as limitation and finitude. An act of freedom is always an act by which we choose some specific thing. Sartre goes even further: freedom is in a sense a lesser kind of being; it is a deficiency, a lack, a sort of gap, a sort of nothingness within being. What is here involved is Sartre's whole doctrine of the for-itself, his whole doctrine of nothingness. I am the being that I am not and I am not the being that I am. Freedom is tied up with my essential negativity (in the Hegelian and dialectical sense of the word as well as the Sartrian sense).

Thirdly, our freedom is a fact; it is part of our facticity, to use the word used by Heidegger and after him by Sartre. Freedom is not self-determined initially; and as it is part of our facticity, we are not free not to choose, we are not free not to be free. This is the import of Sartre's statement that we are condemned to be free. Thus there is not only a facticity but also a necessity to our contingency. We might say—and this would indicate an internal difficulty in Sartre's thought—that it is man's nature to be free, but Sartre rejects the idea of nature properly speaking, and freedom in fact is not a 'nature' since it always affords us the possibility of being something other than what we are.

In the light of what has been said, we see the genesis of the Sartrian idea that we are what we make of ourselves. He appropriates Lequier's precept: *Faire et, en faisant, se faire* (man makes himself). I am the sum total of my acts. We have already contrasted Sartre and Kierkegaard on this point; Sartre, unlike Kierkegaard, does not believe in the ineffable. He holds that we must express ourselves, that we do express ourselves, and that a feeling does not exist apart from its expression. Here Sartre's thought is in line with Hegel's rather than with Kierkegaard's.

We make ourselves. This is what Sartre has sought to show in a good many of his books. In his essay on Baudelaire, for example, he tries to show how Baudelaire *wanted* his defeats in a way, how behind every failure there lurks Baudelaire's will to failure. And from here we can go on to the Sartrian idea that we are always free to accept the judgements of others about ourselves or to refuse them. In this respect again there is a pre-eminence of freedom over my situation. We said a moment ago that the situation only exists through my freedom, since obstacles only exist in relation to the goals I set myself; now we can add that my freedom can choose to recognize or not to recognize the situation.

Another novel feature that Sartre brings to the doctrine of freedom as found in the philosophy of existence in general (except in certain passages in Jaspers) is the interdependence of my freedom and that of others. Their freedom is dependent on mine, and mine on theirs. Nothing could matter to me without mattering to others. Perhaps some sort of analogy could be drawn between this Sartrian notion and the Kantian idea of the universalization of the maxim in the *Critique of Practical Reason*: in choosing a mode of behaviour for myself, I choose it in a way for all men; I decide that all men ought to behave in such and such a fashion. Hence man is responsible not only for himself, but also for others. He is totally responsible not only for his own existence but also for that of others. I cannot will my own freedom without at the same time willing that of others.[1]

Having considered the place of the idea of freedom, we may now try to see the limitations of that idea in each of these philosophies.

It will be seen that freedom which seemed at first to occupy a foremost place in these philosophies is nevertheless dominated in a sense by necessity, by endless struggle against necessity, and is finally transcended by transcendence.

Let us first take Kierkegaard. Kierkegaard believes in human freedom, but on the other hand he believes in grace and affirms a certain co-operation between the two. A new factor, then, is added to the doctrine of freedom. Moreover, in the most profound instances of choice, in the most intense instances of volition, we have a feeling of being unable to act otherwise. Finally, Kierkegaard lays it down—and the other philosophers of existence subscribe to the same position—that we must take our situation upon ourselves. This view is somewhat similar to Nietzsche's 'yea' to destiny, to his *amor fati*. We must accept what we are; we must, after the 'leap' towards transcendence which Kierkegaard would have us make, come back to ourselves and say 'yes' to ourselves. These, then, are the three factors which tend to cut down the scope of freedom in Kierkegaard's thought.

The position of Jaspers is not unlike Kierkegaard's. Jaspers emphasizes the fact that freedom does exist in that intermediate domain which is the domain of existence. But there is for him a domain higher than that of existence, a domain analogous to that of Kierkegaardian grace—the domain of transcendence, and here

[1] But here again there is a difficulty: Is freedom willed? Is it not simply a fact?

there is no more possibility, no more freedom. Freedom vanishes on the threshold of transcendence. It ends in failure precisely because there is beyond existence the domain of transcendence. Freedom is a movement leading to self-negation, to self-efface-ment, so that transcendence may manifest itself. Freedom is the vanishing appearance of transcendence. It vanishes almost as soon as transcendence appears; and as it is itself one of the highest manifestations of Being, it partakes of the characteristic of Being's highest manifestations: it appears only in flashes.

Moreover, in our profoundest acts of freedom, we do not have the feeling of choosing ourselves. When we reach what could be called the highest point of freedom, there is no longer a feeling of choice, but rather the feeling of being unable to will otherwise. Kierkegaard, too, as it was seen, had insisted on this idea. Beyond choice there is something else: there is non-choice, which is superior to choice. In our highest acts of freedom we have the feeling that we are no longer acting alone, that we are impelled by some force no longer wholly our own; and at such times we experience the feeling of having, by our very choice, reached a region where it is no longer possible to choose. This, in the philosophy of Jaspers, is one of the ways in which freedom at its height makes for the appearance of that region where there is no more possibility, no more freedom—the region of transcendence. This is a second factor which, in Jaspers as in Kierkegaard, diminishes the scope of free-dom.

Thirdly, Jaspers stresses the fact that we are 'given' to ourselves. We do not have the feeling of creating ourselves, but are given, 'consigned', as he says, to ourselves; we must receive ourselves, as it were. This constitutes a third factor tending to reduce the place of freedom in Jaspers' thought. It must also be observed that for Jaspers, freedom exists only in relation to something other than itself—in relation to obstacles, in relation to things that deny freedom. Freedom implies non-freedom and struggle against non-freedom. Freedom is inherent to man's nature, to his facticity, and it is a struggle against facticity. That is why it ends in failure in Jaspers' philosophy and perhaps in all the philosophies of exist-ence.

Lastly, the idea of *repetition*, present in Jaspers' thought as in Kierkegaard's and Heidegger's, tends to diminish the scope of freedom; for we must take what we are upon ourselves. It is precisely the given element of myself that I must, it seems, assume, make my own. This idea too helps us to see that the place of freedom is not as preponderant as it would appear at first sight.

We could make parallel observations about Heidegger. For although Heideggerian man is characterized by the ideas of possibility and project, he is also characterized by the fact that his projects have an end—an end not in the sense of goals, but one which puts an end to them: death. And everything, at least in *Sein und Zeit*, is envisaged from the point of view of this end, which is evidently tantamount to the defeat of freedom, since death is defined by Heidegger as the possibility of impossibility or perhaps one might equally say as the impossibility of the possible. This is an inexorable incarnation of facticity—an incarnation which is really a disincarnation. It is only when we are dead that our life becomes a veritable whole according to Heidegger. Thus the idea of boundless freedom ends in failure.

On the other hand, what ought we to do with our freedom? This is where Heidegger's idea of *resolute decision* comes in. We ought—as in Kierkegaard and Jaspers—to say 'yes' to our fate. Here again Heidegger's thought is influenced as much by Nietzsche as by Kierkegaard. Our fate is to live as beings limited by death; we must decide to be what we are—finite beings, limited by death. Once again freedom is submerged by a feeling of necessity.

Our projects are limited by our past. The relation between projects, possibility, the future, on the one hand, and the past and the situation, on the other, raises the problem of idealism vs. realism in Heidegger's philosophy. There is in his philosophy an oscillation between an extreme idealism that accords a central position to freedom and a realism that emphasizes Being—a forsaken and humiliated Being in *Sein und Zeit*. Perhaps some sort of reconciliation between these two tendencies could be conceived if it were granted that truth itself, at least as defined by Heidegger, that is, as consisting in letting Being be what it is, implies a certain freedom; for does not the very word *letting* indicate an act of mind, and in this case the act of a mind no longer humiliated, as it seemed to be in certain passages of *Sein und Zeit*, but simply taking Being in, receiving it; and once again Being predominates. We are on the road to *Holzwege*.

These philosophies which present themselves as philosophies of freedom are perhaps not so freedom-centred as they at first appear to be, and when we come to the philosophy of Sartre, we are confronted with at least two problems concerning the limits of freedom. To begin with, there is the problem raised by the idea of situation. For freedom is always freedom in some given situation; it is limited, conditioned. Thus each of our acts can be interpreted in two ways: in terms of our situation or in terms of our freedom. Then there is the problem of the overall unity of our freedom. Freedom, according to Sartre, is the constant possibility of being something other than what we are. But on the other hand, is there not a fundamental freedom governing all our particular acts of freedom? This question is raised by Sartre in *Being and Nothingness*. Is there not, over and above all our particular projects, some one general project which is *the* project of our life? If the answer is yes, then it would seem that we are committed to the idea of a timeless freedom rather similar to that of Kant and to that proposed by Plato. But then all our particular acts of freedom would depend on this unique and timeless choice. No doubt the original project is rather a general configuration or even a virtual image. Nevertheless the problem remains unsolved.

Lastly, our freedom tends to be self-destructive. It fosters necessity; no sooner is an act performed than it escapes us and turns into an in-itself. But here again we are faced with a number of difficulties: did we not say that according to Sartre we are free always to the same extent? Now we are told that freedom puts fetters upon itself, that the *pour-soi* (for-itself) transforms itself into *en-soi* (in-itself). Did we not say that for Sartre freedom consists in being what one is not and in not being what one is? Now we are told that our past acts weigh down upon us, weigh us down, so to speak. Is not Sartre attributing two rather contradictory characteristics to freedom? Such is our condition says he, that we are at once a freedom which tends to become petrified and a freedom which overcomes, or at least ought to overcome, this petrification, and it is not genuine unless it does overcome the tendency to ossification, the tendency to be what it is when its deeper tendency is to be what it is not.

Freedom is due to nature, since it is our nature to be free; but it is also contrary to nature, since it must continuously try to struggle against its own inner tendency toward petrification, toward transformation into what Sartre calls *in-itself*. Consequently freedom always ends in failure, and, as a matter of fact, it would be more precise to speak of self-liberation than freedom.

In Jaspers too, freedom is caught—caught between nature and transcendence, between two stronger elements which negate it.

But this does not mean that it will fade away. It must, according to Jaspers, exist precisely in this zone of struggle against nature and transcendence. From this point of view, it may be said that we are not free, absolutely speaking, but are engaged in an endless attempt to liberate ourselves.

In Jaspers, freedom disappears on the threshold of transcendence. In Heidegger, it gives way before facticity and necessity. In Jaspers, existence is the impossibility of attaining transcendence and yet an endless hankering after it. In Heidegger, the supreme possibility is the possibility of impossibility, and our greatest act of freedom appears, in some passages at least, to be that in which we recognize that our freedom is overwhelmed by necessity. In Sartre, freedom is always on the verge of disappearing, on the verge of being swallowed up by the in-itself.

It is nevertheless in Sartre that the sense of freedom and the call to freedom remain the strongest, secure from transcendence.

We have seen two triads of categories, the first comprising *existence*, *Being*, and *transcendence*, the second relating to time and including, in the first place, *possibility* and *project*, secondly, *origin* or *source*, and finally, a set of concepts ranging from *now* to *situation* and culminating in the *instant*. We had come to the third triad, whose first term, *choice* and *freedom*, we have studied. We shall now take up the second, composed of *dread* and *nothingness*, and then go on to the third term of this triad: *repetition* and *authenticity*.

It was seen that dread or anguish is, in Kierkegaard, related to the idea of choice. There are possibilities of evil in us. There are temptational possibilities. Hence a first source of dread.

A second source lies in the fact that what is constantly at stake is our eternal salvation or perdition.

The rôle of sin is twofold in Kierkegaard. First, it is consciousness of sin that destroys the Hegelian world view; discontinuous, individual, transcendent, it shatters the System. Nothing, according to Kierkegaard, is more individual, nothing shuts me up more thoroughly in myself than sin. But in the second place, it leads us towards religious existence, since the very idea of sin implies the idea of appearing before God.

The third source of dread consists in this: that it is exceedingly difficult to make out what is good and what is evil, to determine whether a particular possibility is a temptational possibility or a redemptive one. For everything in the province of existence is utterly ambiguous; there are no external signs to help us. And once again we find the recurrent theme of Kierkegaard and Sartre: There are no fast rules, no landmarks; we are navigators without a compass.

The authentic individual, the existent, whom we have sought to portray, will never be sure of being what Kierkegaard calls the Knight of Belief. 'Am I the Knight of Belief' or am I merely tempted?—I cannot say; it is not for me to say; I am here in the region of absolute risk.'

At every moment, Jaspers tells us, I must try to decide whether I am sinking into *nothingness* or whether I am retaining my self-identity by affirming my own existence. I am perpetually caught between the choices of being and non-being. I must decide whether or not I am and what I am. Therefore I am never something that is decided, but always a person who must decide, who is about to decide; shall I remain the same, constant to myself, deeply historical, or shall I abandon myself, uproot myself from my own history?

The ideas of passion and uncertainty are interrelated for Kierkegaard; it is the unsure thing that solicits our passion. We are not impassioned by certainties, but by things involving a risk. The subjective thinker is not in possession of any universalizable truth in the rational sense of the word; rather, he always has the sensation of being in danger, of being on the high seas amid a storm. It is his uncertainty as regards what he believes that heightens and intensifies his subjectivity. He is on a stormy, bottomless sea. In the sphere of existence, in the sphere of subjectivity, there are no proofs, no demonstrations. When he has come to know this risk, the individual is thoroughly transformed; here there are no results in the sense that science gives us results, but the individual is *internally* transformed and, in this sense, everything is transformed.

There is a fourth sense of dread, related to ontology. We already touched upon it when we said that we cannot think of Being, nor yet not think of Being.

Such are the causes of Kierkegaardian dread.

Nor is the rôle of dread less prominent in Jaspers. For Jaspers, what is at stake is not our eternal salvation or perdition, but our existence, and in existence all choices are made independently of objective references.

In Heidegger, too, the idea of dread plays a very important rôle, at least in *Sein und Zeit*. Only by means of dread can we advance from the sphere of the unauthentic to that of the authentic.

Heidegger, like Kierkegaard before him, makes a distinction between dread and fear. Fear always results from particular situations, while dread is our response to the world as such, to the sum total of beings. We experience dread not in connection with any particular thing, but in connection with the world as a whole.

Dread is ever-present for Heidegger as for Kierkegaard. Kierkegaard had said that even the absence of dread is a sign of dread: if a man seems free of dread, he is sure to be hiding his dread from himself through dread of dread. There is never an absence of dread. Dread, in both Kierkegaard and Heidegger, is the bedrock of all our feelings. It is our fundamental feeling. It could be said that in Kant the ontological 'feeling' is of quite a different order: respect is the ontological 'feeling'; the rôle played by respect in Kant is replaced by dread in Kierkegaard and Heidegger.

In his analyses of existence, Heidegger sometimes turns to another feeling, to the feeling of boredom. He believes that boredom reveals our temporal nature, and particularly deep boredom, for he comes to elaborate a whole hierarchy of boredoms: there are particular boredoms, but underlying these there is what he calls deep boredom. It is not difficult to see that deep boredom is nothing other than dread.

Nor is it difficult to see how Heidegger, taking the word 'boredom'—in German *Langeweile*, 'long while'—concludes that the feeling of duration is the foundation of our being.

The same feeling of dread or anguish accompanied by the feeling of nausea, is to be found as the fundamental feeling in Sartre and much for the same reasons as have already been discussed: absence of all objective references, absence of landmarks, the fact that we are in a world where there are no predetermined norms, where we must set up our own norms. We justify all things and consequently we ourselves are unjustifiable. It is this feeling of unjustifiability that permeates Sartre's Orestes and other characters and is the cause of dread.

However, Sartre suggests another source of dread, especially in his lecture *Existentialism is a Humanism*. Dread, Sartre here argues, is caused by the fact that our decisions are never for ourselves alone, but for all men. We have already spoken of this Sartrian notion. By our decisions we commit not only ourselves but all men; hence enormous responsibility is involved in the way we make a decision and in the way we interpret the universe.

In this lecture, then, the idea of dread is accounted for in a rather novel way. But though the accounts may vary—and among the most cogent is the absence of predetermined norms—the feeling of dread is always there as a fundamental theme in the philosophies of existence (exception made of Gabriel Marcel).

From the idea of dread we can pass naturally on to the idea of nothingness. Choice and freedom emerge out of nothingness. Already in Kierkegaard the idea of nothingness was present, tied up to the idea of dread: Temptational possibilities which are intermediate between being and nothingness float before our eyes and make us giddy, fill us with dread.

Nevertheless, the idea of nothingness cannot be said to be central to Kierkegaard's thought. It is true that Kierkegaard could be so interpreted as to stress the rôle of the idea of nothingness in his thought; his feeling of his own nothingness before God, his assertion that God can in no way be characterized are somewhat similar to the Being of negative theologies. None the less, the idea of nothingness is of secondary importance in Kierkegaard if compared with Heidegger; for Kierkegaard, despite what has just been said, was concerned primarily with relative nothingness in the form of possibilities, and not with absolute and actual nothingness.

Heidegger arrives at the idea of nothingness in several ways. First, by the idea, essential to his philosophy, that we are finite beings. Now, the idea of finitude implies the ideas of limitation and nothingness. Secondly, we are brought to an end, terminated, by the last moment of our life, which is death. And here again what we find is the idea of nothingness; it is in the anticipation of death that we come face to face with our own nothingness. In these two ways Heidegger goes from the idea of finitude to the idea of nothingness.

Thirdly, we are, according to Heidegger, always in a state of guilt. We are limited. The idea of limitation is in Heidegger connected to the idea of guilt. Here the question may well be asked whether in Heidegger, as in Jaspers, this idea of guilt is not the vestige of a religious state that they themselves claim to have for the most part left behind.

To exist is to be limited. To be limited is to depart from the absolute and the infinite. Therefore to exist is to be guilty. This idea may be traced back to the Kierkegaardian notion of existence as guilt, but in Kierkegaard the idea is part of a larger doctrine stating that existence is at once the highest value and sin. We are separated from the Wholly Other in relation to whom we live in a state of ceaseless tension. This separation is a guilty thing, but at the same time, this separation is what gives our existence all its intensity and thereby its value.

But the idea of finitude serves merely as a preliminary account of the idea of nothingness in Heidegger. In his essay 'What is Metaphysics ?', Heidegger treats the matter in a much wider and more radical way, contending that every definition, as Spinoza had said, implies a negation. Metaphysics, for instance, is such and such a thing, and that thing only, and not something else. Now, every negation of this kind, according to Heidegger, presupposes nothingness. The error of classical philosophy—and on this score Bergson would also be ranked as a classical philosopher—is that it explains the idea of nothingness in terms of negation. Now, it is the opposite course that we must take. If it were not for the fact that nothingness exists in us, and consequently in the universe, there would be no negation.

But what can we say about nothingness ? We cannot say that it *is*, for that would be a contradictory assertion. We must therefore coin a new word. Nothingness has a certain activity, an activity of negation that Heidegger tries to render by the word to *nought* or to *nihilate*. We are obliged, he believes, to coin new words or rehabilitate words grown obsolete so as to impart certain notions. For instance, it is wrong to say that the world *is*: the world *worlds*. We cannot say that time *is*: it *temporalizes itself*. We cannot say that nothingness *is*: it performs an activity of *noughting* by which it tears things down and reduces them to nought. And, on the other hand, the things that it reduces to nought spring originally from nothingness. Nothingness is therefore the foundation of all things.

The metaphysical question in hand is further complicated by the fact that upon republishing his essay 'What is Metaphysics ?', Heidegger has added a postscript in which he tells us that nothingness is none other than Being. Nothingness can only be defined as that which is no particular being. Now, there is something which is no particular being, namely, Being itself. Heidegger takes it for granted that there cannot be two things having the property—if one can here speak of properties—of not being any particular being. And so he is left with the conclusion that nothingness is Being itself, inasmuch as it defies all determination.

It will be seen that Heidegger's position here borders on negative theology as founded partly on the first hypothesis of Parmenides, elaborated by the Pseudo-Dionysius, and taken up again by the major Christian mystics, and particularly by Eckhart who has had an influence on Heidegger.

It may seem natural here to mention the name of Hegel, as at the beginning of his *Logic* we find the same affirmation that nothingness and Being are one. Hegel believes that if the idea of Being is considered simply and purely, independently of all determination, it will be seen that Being is nothingness. But the Being that Hegel is dealing with at this point in his *Logic* is a purely abstract Being. Therefore, it is to negative theology rather than to Hegel that Heidegger's idea should be compared.

But if Heidegger's own interpretation of his doctrine is accepted, it becomes rather difficult to see how the very concepts of this essay on metaphysics are to be understood, how it can be maintained that Being, since Being and nothingness are now identical, reduces everything to nought, destroys everything. Are we to understand that the world is engulfed, swallowed up by Being? It is not impossible that Heidegger should think so. Nevertheless, between the essay itself and the Appendix, there seem to be some differences and divergencies. And the question remains as to what nothingness is in Heidegger.

It must be admitted that Heidegger's attempt to probe into the nature of nothingness is highly suggestive and significant, one at any rate that has rarely been carried out with so much logic.

In effect one of Plato's conclusions in the *Sophist* was that there can be no absolute nothingness, that there can only be relative nothingnesses, that there can only be Difference. And classical philosophy has always dismissed the idea of absolute nothingness. It is to Heidegger's credit to have tried to show what such an idea of absolute nothingness would consist in. Does he succeed? Perhaps it is not possible to succeed. And so he falls back on the idea that nothingness is Being itself. Being, he says, is all that we have before us. Being reveals and conceals itself at the same time. But what does *concealment* mean? It is difficult to comprehend such a concept as *concealment* without, in one way or another, thinking of negation, and Heidegger tells us that negation cannot be comprehended without nothingness, and the whole problem arises again.

Let us now examine Sartre's doctrine of 'nihilation'. Here the two concepts, existence and nothingness, which were not quite linked in Heidegger, or at least not always in the same way, are linked together. There certainly are passages in Heidegger asserting that it is essentially in *Dasein* that nothingness makes its appearance. But the link between the two ideas is far more rigorous in Sartre. I myself am nothingness; I am the one who introduces the idea of nothingness into the world. The world is plenitude, or rather it would be plenitude were it not for the for-itself, were it not for man. Man is a kind of gap, an empty and vicious duration; it is man that brings *absence* into the world.

It could be said that Sartre often uses the word 'being' as a synonym for 'Being-in-itself', and the word 'nothingness' as a synonym for 'Being-for-itself.' *Being and Nothingness*, the title of his book, stands really for the *in-itself* and the *for-itself*. I, the subject, am nothingness.

But perhaps there is not just one kind of nothingness in Sartre's philosophy; and perhaps his doctrine of nothingness is a regression in comparison, if not with Heidegger's findings, at least with his effort and goal. Heidegger tries, and the attempt, as we said, is significant and suggestive even if not successful, to make us grasp the reality of nothingness.

In Sartre's philosophy there is a multitude of nothingnesses or rather what he calls nihilations. Every psychological phenomenon is interpreted by him in terms of nihilation. Imagination, for example, is that which is not perception; perception, in turn, is that which is not reducible to itself. Each thing, indeed, is nothingness in comparison with something else. For instance, if I wish to achieve some goal, I must set myself an ideal, that is to say, I must nihilate reality; then I must realize my ideal and nihilate once again by my action some aspect of reality. There is a succession, a cascade of nihilations. Every act in the domain of the for-itself constitutes a nihilation.

And so one may wonder whether Sartre does not go back from a Heideggerian conception of nothingness to a Hegelian conception of nothingness—for Hegel firmly regarded mind, which underlies everything, as negativity—and even further back to a Platonic conception. Behind the Sartrian idea of nothingness what we find is the idea of otherness.

The ideas of *dread* and *nothingness* make it possible for us to advance from the unauthentic to the authentic. The two concepts of *unauthenticity* and *authenticity*, found above all in Heidegger, are also central to Kierkegaard's thought.

Heidegger makes a distinction between the domain of One (*Man*), that is to say the domain of our being in so far as we are replaceable by any other human being, and another domain to which we accede only after experiencing dread.

Heidegger says that when he speaks of authenticity and unauthenticity, he does not mean to imply a superiority of the one over the other, that they are both metaphysical categories, and that as metaphysical facts they are of equal importance. Actually, it is difficult to follow him on this score, for no sooner does one differentiate between authenticity and unauthenticity than one becomes deferential to authenticity.

We come now to the ideas of *failure (échec)* and *repetition*.

In Kierkegaard's case there is failure in his very life, and it is to overcome this failure that he resorts to God, turns to transcendence. It is the consciousness of the failure of geniuses—be it Kierkegaard, or Nietzsche, or Van Gogh—that leads Jaspers to consider the category of failure as essential to the philosophy of existence. It is through failure that, as we noted, the existent may approach transcendence. We noted also that Jaspers' philosophy may be regarded both as an ontology of failure and as a failure of ontology, since he fails to achieve a unified idea of Being.

The idea of failure is also to be found in Sartre, for example in connection with the individual's relations with others.

Now, to overcome failure there is according to Kierkegaard a way, which he propounds in a highly complex and confused fashion in the work called *Repetition*. This idea of repetition, by which Kierkegaard hoped to turn failure into triumph, has remained one of the existential categories of the philosophies of existence.

What does Kierkegaard mean by repetition? In a period of his life previous to that in which his thought crystallized, Kierkegaard was firmly convinced that we can be happy only if we can recapture a given moment of the past exactly as it was lived. This Kierkegaardian idea is somewhat similar to Proust's ambition in *A la Recherche du Temps Perdu*: to really recapture some moment of the past is to achieve happiness. And in a rather puerile fashion, it seems, Kierkegaard had attempted repetition, for example by returning to the opera-house to hear his favourite opera, so as to put himself in exactly the same state of mind as that in which he had heard it for the first time. But he came to realize that this was an impossible task. His relations with his fiancée decided the matter, and he finally concluded that it is not in this world that repetition is possible, but in the next, and through faith. Nevertheless, he added: once we have found faith we can perhaps achieve repetition even in this world. Is not Job, for example, said to have found his family and his sons again in the end? Consequently, this world can be rendered hallow precisely by our renunciation of it.

Kierkegaard would therefore have us distinguish between a primary immediation, which is prior to reflection and faith, and what he calls matured immediation—mediated immediation, we might call it, using the phrase of his archenemy, Hegel—which one would attain after having been in contact with transcendence. Only after living this instant which is the encounter of time and eternity can one really regard this world as hallowed.

Kierkegaard's final aim, then, is not to get away from this world through religion, but to return to the world, the world as it is, and even not to differ from other men; the man who has a great faith, Kierkegaard believes, will in no way differ from others, will rejoice like them, and the ideal would perhaps be that his faith will not be known to others; he will have transfigured the real world in such a way that he himself will on the face of it not differ from those who bestow all their confidence upon the real world.

When we come to Heidegger the idea of repetition cannot be interpreted or accounted for in the same way, for in Heidegger, at least in *Sein und Zeit*, there is no allusion to any godhead. We are in this world limited in our very being. The only way to take our destiny upon ourself—for this finally is the meaning of the Heideggerian decision—is to want ourselves to be limited by death. It is therefore by way of dread and the thought of death that we arrive at repetition. We must take what we are upon ourselves. This is what Heidegger calls the anticipatory resolute decision by which we live our own death in advance. We overcome our failure by becoming conscious of that failure.

Jaspers' interpretation of the idea of *repetition* is different from Heidegger's and a little closer to Kierkegaardian repetition: our failures, he believes, are nothing but the affirmation of transcendence; they are the reverse side of transcendence. The fact that we fail is an indication that there is some greater thing, a sphere higher than that of existence. We become aware of this sphere in what Jaspers calls boundary situations.

Thus, failure makes it possible for us to mount from existence towards transcendence, and for this reason, in so far as it conducts us to repetition, it is the supreme 'cipher', the supreme symbol of transcendence.

Through failure, Jaspers believes, we attain being, for in failure we attain something that is in no way reducible to ourselves; we see glittering at a distance something greater than ourselves. Only for an instant do we see it glitter, for that which is higher than all else is necessarily precarious; the symbol of transcendence reveals itself only in flashes, flashes in the night, but these flashes account for everything.

It is thus seen that the two ideas of failure and repetition are not so opposed as they seem at first, since in both Heidegger and Jaspers it is failure that brings about the possibility of repetition, it is failure that leads us to triumph and to authenticity.

Nietzsche tells us that the world in which we find ourselves is an absurd one since all things will recur exactly as they are. The superman is the man who can stand this vision, depressing to others, and can affirm and even will the eternal recurrence of things. The man who says 'yea' to life and says it eternally and does not retract it even if life recurs in this absurd fashion—such a man will have triumphed over pessimism, over Schopenhauerism; he will have achieved love of destiny. Now, this Nietzschean idea is evidently present, and intimately so, in the thought of Heidegger and Jaspers.

We have come to the end of this triad which consisted of the following categories: first, *choice* and *freedom*; second, *nothingness* and *dread*; third, *repetition* and *authenticity*.

IV

The Unique - The Other - Communication

WE shall now take up a fourth triad of concepts comprising the ideas of the *Unique*, the *Other*, and *communication*.

Kierkegaard says that it is always to the isolated and unique individual that he addresses himself. In this he may be compared to Stirner and Nietzsche. No other philosopher, says Kierkegaard speaking of himself, has put so much emphasis on the concept of the individual, of the Unique one. And, as we have seen, it was on the basis of this concept that he opposed Hegelianism. The individual is not reducible to any system; he is not just a moment in the history of the System; he is not expressible by his works. For Hegel the individual is the sum total of his acts and works, and parallel assertions can be found in Sartre. But for Kierkegaard, as we saw, the individual has secrets that cannot be communicated. This is Kierkegaard's germinal and central insight.

In the province of existence, Kierkegaard believes, the individual can only hear his own voice; he cannot, properly speaking, join the society of other men; he must take his secret to the grave. But it is exceedingly difficult to expose doctrinally the category of the Unique one. 'This category,' says Kierkegaard, 'cannot form the subject of a dissertation; it is a power and a task.'

In the defiles of belief the door is opened to the individual and closed behind him. Never are we as alone as in our confrontation with God.

If Kierkegaard asks the individual to be unique this does not mean that he should develop his individuality in a direction wholly different from that of others. There is a radical difference between an aesthetic determination, like that of the romantic genius, and a moral determination.

The idea of the Unique is also present in Jaspers, under the twofold influence of Nietzsche and Kierkegaard. We have already mentioned the importance of the idea of choice in Jaspers' thought, and it is by way of the idea of choice that the concept of the Unique may best be approached in Jaspers. The Unique is the existent as he is and chooses himself before transcendence.

In Gabriel Marcel we find the idea, if not of the Unique, at least of irreducibility: the problems of existence, according to Marcel, are those that are not reducible to intellectual terms.

But face to face with the Unique there is in all these philosophies, in one form or another, what we may call the Other. It was already seen that in Kierkegaard God is called the Wholly Other. The Wholly Other is that which is infinitely above us, and we are what we are, we exist, only because there is such a transcendence.

Kierkegaard is concerned at the same time with the problem of *others* and one of the questions we shall discuss in connection with the idea of communication is this: how can we tell others that the Wholly Other exists?

In the domain of subjectivity there is something else besides the individual in the first person singular. Great as his solitude may be, Kierkegaard carries on a sort of passionate dialogue: there is a second person, the person he addresses, and over and above the first and second persons there is God, conceived not as a *he*, but in such a way as to render possible, by invocation and prayer, the relationship between the first person and the second. For Kierkegaard all true love is grounded in the love of God.

It is already evident that our first two categories—the Unique and the Other—cannot be discussed without the third: communication. The problem of communication is one with which Kierkegaard was greatly concerned.

How can we communicate our subjective knowledge to others? Kierkegaard believes that we cannot communicate it directly; we can only communicate it in roundabout ways, by a sort of dissimulation, so as to 'seduce the others towards the truth'. The mind can reveal itself only indirectly, for no outward sign can completely reveal the inner state. There will always remain a residue of secrets. Moreover, certainty is impossible in this matter. And indirect communication alone can preserve the freedom of the other person; in a 'passionate tension' the other will be able to make the truth his own.

Kierkegaard worked out what he calls the theory of indirect communication, which probably responds to some deep aspect of his own personality, for he has the feeling that he cannot give direct utterance to what he thinks. He must resort to roundabout ways, and that is what he does when he has to break his engagement. Thus, indirect communication is a psychological necessity for Kierkegaard, but, according to him, it is also a necessity of the times for the religious writer exposing his religion. (It would be of no avail to tell people directly: 'Become Christian'.) Hence Kierkegaard took detours, describing first the aesthetic experience, showing why it can hardly be satisfactory and why it must make way for the ethical experience. And at least one of his books seems to have been written with the intention of showing that the individual must become part of society by finding a vocation in life, by getting married, and so forth. But above the aesthetic experience as above the ethical experience, there is religious experience proper, and this is what Kierkegaard propounds, particularly in *Fear and Trembling* by the example of Abraham.

These, then, are two reasons, one psychological, the other related to the feebleness of religious feelings in modern times, which cannot be aroused directly, for indirect communication. A third reason is that indirect communication alone preserves the freedom of the other person and at the same time allows us to see the extent to which the other person is free, to see the quantity, if one may so call it, of freedom which is in the other person.

But the idea of indirect communication has a still greater import in Kierkegaard's thought: God himself did not communicate directly with humanity; he came disguised, he came incognito; he did not choose to reveal himself directly; he chose to reveal himself indirectly.

Thus indirect communication, which stemmed from Kierkegaard's own psychological experience and from the necessities of the communication of religious truth, is finally ascribed to God himself and to the relation between God and man.

The idea of indirect communication is related to another idea, that of *misunderstanding*. Indeed, between God and man, as is shown by the life and death of Christ, there is, according to Kierkegaard, an immense misunderstanding. And the idea of misunderstanding dominates Kierkegaard's whole psychological life. Here again his religious conception and his psychological experience correspond.

But in the last years of his life Kierkegaard went beyond indirect communication. When he rose against what he called the Established Church, against the Lutheran Church of Denmark, he said: I must speak out; I must express myself directly; I must tell the truth in the most direct way possible. But except at the very end, Kierkegaard believed in indirect communication.

The idea of indirect communication is also found in a certain way in Jaspers. For transcendence, which is higher than man, cannot form the subject of direct communication. Jaspers reiterates that the transcendent cannot be talked about except by tautologies, antinomies, antitheses and finally by *petitio principii* and nonsense. His position here is parallel to negative theology. That which is higher than all else cannot be talked about, cannot form the subject of direct communication.

Nevertheless, Jaspers allows for the possibility of direct communication to a far greater extent than Kierkegaard. But even as regards Kierkegaard, we have perhaps not given enough attention to the importance he accords to love. One of the volumes of his sermons is called *Works of Love*. He believes in a certain direct communication between God and His creatures, even if he insists in the first instance on God's incognito and His misunderstanding with His creatures. There is what Kierkegaard calls the Invisible Church; we can become united with others; there is a domain which Buber and Marcel were to call the domain of 'Thou', which is the domain of the relationship between man and man.

This is what Jaspers insists upon when he speaks of love in struggle or the struggle of love; for it must not be imagined— Scheler had already pointed this out—that love is a fusion of two souls; each remains itself; and according to Jaspers, who differs from Scheler on several aspects of this doctrine, each soul has to struggle against the soul of the being it loves. The two form one another by a kind of creative combat.

The ideas we have been discussing are of less importance in Heidegger, but it must nevertheless be said that it is unfair to charge Heidegger with disregarding the union between men, for the Heideggerian *Sein* is always also *Mitsein*: to be is to be with.

It has been said that Heidegger exemplifies this 'being with' primarily by work. But it will be seen, for example in his commentaries on Hölderlin's poems, that love and direct communication are also given a place in Heidegger's philosophy.

Thus we see that the problem of communication between man and man, which is rather insignificant—at least as a problem—in classical philosophies, is highly significant in the philosophies of existence, even if these philosophies do not admit a thoroughly direct communication—direct in the usual sense of the word—with others. Kierkegaard's personal difficulty in communicating with others is one of the sources of importance given to the problem of communication. What was taken for granted in classical philosophies becomes a problem in the philosophies of existence.

Sartre seems to imply, when he speaks of love and communication in *Being and Nothingness*, that communication is always awkward or abortive. The individual needs love, according to Sartre, mainly for the purpose of self-justification; he feels justified because he is appreciated by another. But, on the other hand, Sartre has a very strong feeling that no sooner do we feel the glance of another than that other takes hold of our world, as it were, which hitherto belonged to ourselves alone. No sooner do I feel looked at than I am robbed of myself and my world by the glance of the other. And our relationship with others is in Sartre's novels and plays held to be the cause of our unhappiness. 'Hell is others.'

The reason for this, according to Sartre, is that what we really want is to possess the other in his freedom, and this is something of a contradiction. For a person may be free, or on the other hand, he may be possessed. But he cannot be free and possessed at the same time; we cannot possess a person in his freedom.

Moreover, love as described in *Being and Nothingness* is always tempted by the in-itself; it tends to make us slip from the for-itself into the in-itself, tends to make objects out of us.

The question may be asked whether Sartre considers satisfactory communication impossible also in the world of authenticity or whether he confines it to the world of unauthenticity. In his book on Sartre, Jeanson maintains, and largely with reason, that Sartre's description of love in *Being and Nothingness* applies only to un-authentic love and not to profound love, which originates and ends in moments of authenticity.

We have seen that all these philosophies consider communication far from easy. Communication is indirect, is a struggle in Kierkegaard and Jaspers; it is awkward and abortive in Sartre. But in this matter as in several others, we must make an exception of Gabriel Marcel as well as of Buber and Berdyaev; for Marcel affirms the possibility and reality of communication, of religious communication, that is to say, communication of the 'I' with the 'absolute Thou', and also of communication with others, which is founded, for Gabriel Marcel, on the religious communication with the 'absolute Thou'. There are values, values of fidelity and of hope, which depend on communication, which do not exist without the reality of communication; the 'we' is as real as the 'I'.

Love, says Gabriel Marcel, always bears on an infinity; it is tied to a feeling of inexhaustibility, of 'evermore'. Marcel contrasts on the one hand the 'I' and the 'thou', on the other, the 'he'. The 'he' forms the sphere of judgements, the 'I' and the 'thou', the sphere of appeal, of invocation, of prayer.

Thus, one may contrast Gabriel Marcel with Sartre, the Sartre at least of *Being and Nothingness*. Whereas Sartre says that the glance of another robs us of something, Gabriel Marcel believes that there are glances which have the power of revealing us to ourselves, of revealing the other, of revealing the world. The world after such a glance becomes a world of appeals and prayers and invocations.

Belief and love are in effect not judgements essentially, but appeal and invocation. To believe, according to Marcel, means always to believe in a 'thou', a 'thou' that seems unique to us. But when it is the 'absolute Thou', then what is involved is no longer love, or rather it is that love which is belief.

Love, then, is a refusal to call the 'thou' into question and transform him thereby into a 'he'. (Quite similar ideas are to be found in Kierkegaard.) The 'thou', says Gabriel Marcel, is to invocation what the subject is to judgement. There is here a sort of creative fidelity, for it creates that in which it believes. Hence the idea of consecration; hence also the importance of the ideas of hope and faith in Gabriel Marcel.

Gabriel Marcel forbids us, as it were, to question our own deepest feelings. For such questioning would transform *the mystery* into a *problem*, into a question, doing away with *the mystery* as such. But what then is to be done with the 'dialectic of certainty and uncertainty' which (along with obedience) constitutes love according to Kierkegaard? The question remains as to what extent the object of belief and the believer can be separated from one another. No doubt Marcel's ideas call for some sort of theory of relations which he has not elaborated fully. In his case the same question comes up that came up in connection with Kierkegaard: to what extent is the object of belief independent of the believer? Kierkegaard tells us: between the Absolute and me there is absolutely no relation. And, on the other hand, he tells us: between the Absolute and me there is an intense relation. How can both statements be true?

Let us recall that in his first philosophical work, *Journal Métaphysique*, Gabriel Marcel's position was very close to a negative theology; it contained profound formulas such as this: 'As soon as you speak of God, you are no longer speaking of God.'

V

Truth-Subjectivity - Truth-Being - Multiplicity of Truths

WE have examined what we called the main categories of existence: first *existence, Being, transcendence;* then the categories relating to time—*possibility* and *project, origin,* and *now, situation, instant;* thirdly *choice* and *freedom, nothingness* and *dread, repetition* and *authenticity;* fourthly, the *Unique,* the *Other,* and *communication.* We would now like to discuss two final triads, one concerning *truth,* the other relating to *paradox.*

Truth in Kierkegaard appears essentially as subjectivity. In Jaspers we shall find a theory of multiplicity of truths, and in Heidegger a theory attempting to identify truth and Being. Thus, we can follow through a movement going from truth-subjectivity to truth-Being.

What does Kierkegaard mean by the statement: truth is subjectivity? According to Hegel, the business of the philosopher is to identify himself with the absolute Mind in its successive incarnations; he must trace out—and this is what Hegel does in his *Phenomenology* and with a different approach in his *Logic*—the various steps that the mind takes in going either from perception to the absolute Reality or from the abstract idea of Being once again to the absolute Reality.

To understand truth, according to Kierkegaard, is to appropriate it for oneself, to produce it, and at the same time to be infinitely interested in it. Kierkegaard's thought is dominated by the idea of an infinite concern about oneself.

For Hegel, truth is to be gained by following the transformations of the Idea—transformations which result from the mechanism or dynamism of thesis, antithesis, and synthesis. With each transformation there appears a moment higher than the preceding one—what Hegel calls the truth of the preceding moment. So that the truth of a moment of mind always lies in the moment that follows, leading finally to the totality which contains all the successive moments and which is the absolute Idea. At that point we shall have gone beyond time, we shall have really lived the eternity of the Idea, we shall have entered upon absolute philosophy.

Kierkegaard is radically opposed to such a conception. I live at a particular moment in time, and my business is not to identify myself, in a way that to Kierkegaard would be sacriligious, to the totality of moments of time; I must assume my position in time; I am a finite individual and must not attempt to measure up to eternity.

What am I to do? I must strive and strain towards what I shall call truth. And truth for Kierkegaard is essentially God in His Incarnation, Jesus Christ, who said Himself: 'I am the Truth.' And when the God-man that is Christ says: 'I am the Truth', He comes to us as a scandal, as a paradox, and it is in this tension that we must place ourselves in order to understand that the *Infinite* incarnated itself, that is to say, embodied itself in a *finite* form; it is this tension that permits us to attain truth, for truth lies essentially in the intensity of our relation to the thing in which we believe. Here we meet again Kierkegaard's doctrine of *how*, about which we have already said a word. It is not the *what*, it is not the dogma, that constitutes truth; it is my attitude towards the dogma.

Thus Kierkegaard's precept is: 'Be subjective, and you will be within truth.'

The subjective thinker, says Kierkegaard, unites eternity and time; he himself is the union of eternity and time, since he conceives eternal truth but conceives it at a particular instant in time. He himself is therefore a paradox.

Belief, Jaspers tells us, is a movement of existence, is 'the certainty of the being of love'. Kierkegaard defines it as the voice of the Divinity, as a battle with God, signifying by this the movement and affirmation of the existent outside of any objective guarantees, acting in accordance with his origin and in an unconditional manner.

However, this idea has to be completed; there is a Kierkegaardian dialectic which places man, essentially finite, at once in the domain of truth and in the domain of falsehood; man cannot render himself adequate before God; he is guilty, and it is only through his feeling of guilt that he can advance to the religious sphere.

But for the moment let us take the following as the first conclusion about truth in the philosophy of existence: truth is subjectivity.

But let us note, too, that from the very beginning of the philosophy of existence, truth is also identified with Being. Jesus is Being. All belief is belief in Being.

Here as in other facets of his philosophy, Jaspers tries to arrive at a more general conception, while preserving the Kierkegaardian conception. There is, he says, no doubt truth as it was conceived by Kierkegaard and at times by Nietzsche. But there are other forms of truth. There is the truth of the empirical domain; there is the truth of the scientific domain. These, too, are truths.

Jaspers attempts to show that the idea of truth varies from one human discipline to another, that these various truths are at war with each other, and that each attains its true worth only by its struggle against the others. Thus, truth-subjectivity achieves its full worth only because there is a truth-objectivity with which it must join battle.

Hence we must always, in dealing with the question of truth, decide in which domain we wish to define it, and Kierkegaard's theory is thus integrated into a larger whole.

Moreover, Jaspers insists on the bond between truth and Being: on this point he is at times close to Heidegger. The idea of truth cannot be separated from the idea of Being, Heidegger tells us. Philosophers have been wrong to look for truth in judgements. Judgements always refer, says Heidegger, following Husserl's phenomenological theory, to something other than themselves, and prior to themselves, namely Being. And only in reference to Being is there truth in a judgement. Consequently, from the truth of judgements, which is a secondary truth, we must go back to a primary truth, which is the truth of Being. Heidegger likes to point out that the word ἀλήθεια, by which the Greeks designated truth, is composed of the privative prefix ἀ and ληθεια which comes from the verb λανθάνιν which has the same root as the name of the river Lethe. Ἀλήθεια, therefore, is that which is unveiled, that which is not hidden. If we reflect on the word αλήθεια, we shall, according to Heidegger, see that the Greeks felt that truth for man is something that is initially in a hiding-place whence it must be dislodged.

Thus—and we have already encountered this from a different point of view in Kierkegaard—man is in error or at fault by his very nature as a finite being.

But wherein lies truth? It is, Heidegger declares, in beings. It is not in judgements; all we have to do is to reveal it. Thus it is that there is a truth which is identical with Being, and that truth, according to Heidegger, is the light of Being. We are in the light of Being and in the darkness of error.

Concerning the idea of truth, then, we can see a kind of dialectic proceeding from truth-subjectivity, as elaborated by Kierkegaard, to truth-Being, as elaborated by Heidegger, and passing through truth-multiplicity as propounded by Jaspers.

But on the other hand, it must not be thought that Heidegger's theory is completely opposed to Kierkegaard's, for if in Heidegger we can come to the idea of Being, it is after all through *Dasein*, through existence, that we can do so; it is therefore by setting out from truth as we feel it in ourselves that we can go towards truth-Being. It is through existence that we can arrive at Being.

VI

Paradox - Tension - Ambiguity

WE come now to the last triad of categories, composed of *paradox, tension,* and *ambiguity.* We have already insisted on the idea of paradox in connection with existence. And from the idea of paradox we can proceed easily to that of tension.

The Kierkegaardian dialectic differs from the Hegelian in that it is individual, passionate, and discontinuous, proceeding by sudden leaps, by crises. 'Man,' he says, 'is a synthesis whose opposite extremes must be kept intact.' He wants to maintain the thesis and the antithesis without letting them pass into a synthesis which would really spell their annihilation. And so the antithesis is to remain present in the thesis, as uncertainty is present in belief, as that over which I triumph is present at the moment of my triumph.

The existent is a man who is the battleground of contrary tendencies; he is a man who unites in himself the different ages of life by an existential contemporaneousness, who unites the pathetic, the dialectic, and the comic in an indissoluble moment.

But we can remark that it is not so much the ideas of paradox and tension and dialectic that are present, for example, in Sartre and Merleau-Ponty as the idea of ambiguity. In his *Phenomenology of Perception* and in what he writes on behaviour, Merleau-Ponty throws into relief the idea of ambiguity. And for Sartre, as we saw in our discussion of freedom, there is always some ambiguity between the interpretation of our acts in terms of the situation and the interpretation of the same acts in terms of freedom. There are different possible interpretations, different possible decipherments of human acts, and we are free to choose, and at the same time in a situation to choose, some particular interpretation. The history of the philosophies of existence may be represented as going from the ideas of paradox and tension to the idea of ambiguity. What used to be central to existential thought was the affirmation of contact between antithetical terms: finite and infinite, temporal and eternal. Today, it is the affirmation of a diversity of interpretations; the human condition is such, it is said, that the same phenomena may be interpretated in a variety of ways. No doubt in going from the idea of a paradox to that of ambiguity existential thought loses some of its acuity; but perhaps on the other hand it gains in amplitude.

VII

Comprehensive View

WE can now glance back at the different categories that we have enumerated. We shall be able to see better what the individual existent is in so far as he is the actual subject of the philosophy of existence.

The existent is oriented towards possibility; he *is* choice, freedom, projects, uniqueness, subjective truth, paradox.

But on the other hand, the existent exists only because there is something else beside him; this is what we designated by the three terms—essentially different from one another, but all three opposed to existence—Being, nothingness, and the Other. The existent exists only because there are other things beside him: because there is Being which the existent tries to seize in thought without ever fully succeeding; because there is nothingness from which the existent emerges and into which he dissolves in a sense in Sartre's philosophy; because there is the Other with whom the existent communicates.

We also saw the feelings that accompany the existent, feelings of dread and tension.

We saw, too, the categories that bring into union the various existential terms: transcendence, effecting a union between existence and Being; situation, effecting a union between the future and the past; communication, effecting a union between the existent and the Other.

All the essential existential concepts could be traced back to the influence of Kierkegaard. The idea of solitude, of dread, the idea of subjectivity, of forlornness, even that of care, the importance accorded to time, to possibility, to project, the idea of nothingness, the idea of paradoxical relations—all this is to be found in Kierkegaard's meditations.

Every philosophy has a certain number of terms that it has forged or appropriated for itself; every philosophy possesses a vocabulary of its own. The Cartesian speaks of clear and distinct ideas, of evidence; the Kantian of *a priori* synthesis, of pure reason. Let us try to compile a short existentialist vocabulary:

Ambiguity	Failure	Risk
Antinomy	Finitude	Scandal
Authenticity	Freedom	Secret
Care	Future	Sin
Choice	Guilt	Situation
Communication	Historicity	Solitude
Contingency	Instant	Subjectivity
Contradiction	Leap	Thou
Death	Nothingness	Transcendence
Despair	Origin	Trembling
Dialectic	Otherness	Uncertainty
Dread	Paradox	Unique
Exception	Possibility	World
Existence	Project	
Facticity	Repetition	

It is true that some of these categories figure less in Gabriel Marcel. This could be historically explained to a certain extent by the fact that Marcel's thought developed independently of Kierkegaard's. And it could also be explained by the fact that the religious solution is accompanied and prepared far less by dread in Marcel than in Kierkegaard. The ideas of dread and nothingness do not play as important a rôle in Gabriel Marcel as in the other philosophers that we have classed along with him as philosophers of existence.

What can we say now about the general character of the philosophies of existence? We recalled at the beginning E. Brehier's observation, which helped us to seek out the origins of these philosophies: metaphysical empiricism and anxiety.

In a book on existentialism by an American author, Mrs. Grene, there is the following sentence: 'Existentialism is an attempt to grasp human nature in human terms without resorting to the superhuman or to what could be called the subhuman.' In other words, the philosophies of existence—and Mrs. Grene is mainly concerned with Sartre's philosophy—are an attempt to explain man independently of purely scientific categories, on the one hand, and purely religious categories, on the other. Existentialism rejects the excuses that materialism can give, or seems able to give; it rejects, too, the aid and refuge offered by supernaturalism and religion. There can be no purely materialistic explanation and therefore no excuse for our responsibility; nor can there be any refuge outside this world.

From a rather similar standpoint one could note, particularly in Sartre's philosophy, an attempt to attribute to man what is ordinarily attributed to God alone.

Perhaps the point should not be laboured; nevertheless it can be remarked that, for example, essence and existence, which theologians say are one in God, are now said to be one even in man.

Moreover, it is said that man *is* freedom and that this freedom knows, as it were, no limits. And curiously enough, in his Preface to the *Morceaux Choisis de Descartes*, Sartre tells us that Descartes really wished to attribute an unlimited freedom to man, that the freedom he attributed to God is the freedom he would have liked to attribute to man, but that he did not succeed in doing so. Historically viewed, the interpretation is highly questionable. Nevertheless, it is useful as an insight into Sartre's own tendency; for the urge that he attributes to Descartes he probably felt in himself: the need to give man the greatest possible freedom is undoubtedly one of the driving forces of Sartrian philosophy.

Thirdly, it is said that man is the source of all value judgements.

Thus, in these three respects, it may be said that Sartre's existentialism tends to put man in the place of God.[1]

But if man is endowed with qualities that traditional philosophy reserved for God, he is nevertheless said to be a failure as a God; for to be a full God he would indeed have to achieve a union between the in-itself and the for-itself, and such a union is declared impossible by Sartre.

We might inquire into the causes of the popularity of the philosophies of existence. No doubt it was due first of all to the rejection of other philosophies and the consciousness of their bankruptcy. It must furthermore be borne in mind that after the turmoil of the war and the Occupation there was an urge to rally about a doctrine,

[1] What has been said of Sartre is not true of the other forms of existential philosophy: not true of Jaspers, who speaks of transcendence, of a domain higher than man; nor of Gabriel Marcel evidently; nor of Heidegger, who says that beyond man there is the domain of Being and that man exists only by virtue of his contact with Being.

and the newer the doctrine the better; in this respect, it may be said that 'existentialism' assumed the same rôle that surrealism had assumed after the preceding war. In the third place, no philosophy, save that of Nietzsche, had put forward so emphatically the idea that man is the creator of all values. And it is certain that the importance given to freedom and the idea that our freedom persists in all circumstances contributed to the fame of these philosophies. On this point, one could to some extent compare the initial cause of the popularity of Sartre's philosophy to that of the popularity of Stoicism.

The very ambiguities of existentialist thought, at least as they are found in Sartre, have contributed to its impact. What appeared to be a pessimistic philosophy first in *Nausea* and even in *Being and Nothingness* turned with *The Flies*, for example, or with some of Sartre's political studies, into a doctrine of hope.

F. Alquié has shown how this philosophy, by its very ambiguity, by some of its contradictions, is characteristic of modern man and perhaps of the human condition in general.

The philosophies of existence must not be conceived of as a series of philosophical dogmas. Man is the being that calls his own existence into question, puts it at stake, puts it into danger. Existence is a self-questioning thing. Man is the being that is a philosopher by his very being.

But as man is bound to the world, in putting himself into question, he puts into question the world which he develops about himself in some way. If for Heidegger the first definition of philosophy is an inquiry into Being by the being that we are, the second definition, based on the etymology that Heidegger attributes to the word 'philosophy', would be 'the wisdom of love' (and not, as is ordinarily said, the love of wisdom), if by wisdom we mean our communion with the world. To philosophize is to be versed in the love of Being and the world. Philosophy, then, is according to Heidegger the knowledge of being-in-the-world—not only of the existent in so far as he is oriented towards his future, and as he is defined by Kierkegaard, but of the existent in so far as he stands in an ecstatic relation with the world. Thus, there is no longer a subject facing an object; we must destroy the classical concept of subject in order to understand that we are always outside ourselves, this expression itself ceasing, as we said, to have a clear meaning since there is no longer a *we* that we are outside of.

In calling himself into question, man calls into question the entire universe which is bound to him. In every philosophical question the totality of the world is involved, even as the individual's existence is risked as a supreme stake. Thus we find the ideas of individuality and totality constantly united.

It could likewise be said that the ideas of individuality and generality are joined. Heidegger, in fact, does not speak for a particular individual, but for all individuals. He describes human existence in general. Dread is no doubt a particular experience, but through it we arrive at the general conditions of existence, at what Heidegger calls *existentialia*. Heidegger would have us distinguish his philosophy from Kierkegaard's by this: that Kierkegaard always remains in the *Existenziell* whereas Heidegger attains the *Existenzial*, that is to say, the general characteristics of human existence. The question may well be asked whether in doing so Heidegger does not reintroduce the idea of essence into his philosophy, whether Kierkegaard is not more constant to existential thinking in banishing the idea of essence. In other words, the question may be asked whether the search for *existentialia* is compatible with the affirmation of existence.

Naturally, a philosophy such as Kierkegaard's poses many problems. On the one hand, does he not after all attempt to rationalize and to explain the paradox by presenting it as the union of the finite and the infinite ? And although he purports to show us a scandal to reason, does he not give a sort of justification to the scandal, which would ultimately do away with the scandal as such ? On the other hand, Kierkegaard himself says that the coming of Christ into the world, in the manner in which it took place, does not constitute the supreme paradox; for the supreme paradox would require that no one notice the coming of God. 'I meditate on this problem,' he writes, 'and I am bewildered by it.' Let us add that the paradox exists only for those who inhabit this earth. For the Blessed, that is to say for those who see the truth, the paradox vanishes. In other words, these considerations are only valid in relation to man's existence here below.

VIII

The Ultimate Problems of the Philosophies of Existence

RESPECTIVE VALUE OF THEIR VARIOUS FEATURES

BUT perhaps all this does not amount to objections. It is very difficult to determine whether such observations are objections or whether, by accentuating the paradox, they reinforce the Kierkegaardian conception. The same is true of the questions raised by the relations between subjectivity and history, the intensity of the subjective feeling being based, paradoxically, on a historical and objective fact. The same is true, again, of the relations between eternity and history, for if the moment of Incarnation is an eternal moment with which we must continually be contemporary, the paradox is likely to vanish.

Perhaps with the objections that philosophers such as Reuter and Käte Nadler and Etienne Gilson address to Kierkegaardian thought, we come, on the other hand, to a set of criticisms which, should they prove valid, would undermine the very possibility of such thought. 'Kierkegaardian existentialism of subjectivity does not side-step the common necessity of operating with essences; it simply creates new ones of which it could be said that they take refuge in a particularly ferocious manner behind their essential purity. The pure faith of subjective existentialism is one such essence, and the history of religious thought hardly knows any other that objects more strenuously to all participation.' 'Such oppositions are ordinarily the product of abstract thought, and it may be asked whether, at the very moment when Kierkegaard passionately spurned the confusion between abstraction and existence, he did not treat existence as a new abstraction, one whose essence required that it make an abstraction of all abstraction.' It is seen by the end of the quotation that what is at stake here is the possibility of a war on abstractions; the conflict is then between Kierkegaard's thought, affirming the possibility of an existent essence whose abstraction is a felt abstraction, and a thought of a rational order.

We might now try to make some critical remarks about the philosophies of existence.

We could distinguish different elements, that enter into these philosophies. For the first thing to note is that the philosophy of existence is rather heterogeneous, composite. In the philosophy of existence in its various forms there are elements that are properly existential. Those are the ones we dwelt upon when we said that they are retraceable to Kierkegaard. There are phenomenological elements deriving from Husserl and found particularly in Heidegger and Sartre. There are Hegelian elements. There are ontological elements, and these we shall take up first.

The philosophies of existence attach great importance to the idea of Being. The idea of Being was already present in Kierkegaard's thought, but it occupies a much more prominent position, a much more explicit position in the philosophies of Heidegger and Jaspers. For all the philosophers of existence, philosophy is essentially the study of Being. Heidegger is particularly insistent on this point, and a little reflection on the title of Sartre's book, *Being and Nothingness*, will reveal the importance of the idea of Being in Sartre's philosophy.

But what can we say about the idea of Being in these philosophies? We can describe it as a state of dispersion, a state of non-unity. All we find—and we already dwelt upon this point—are categories of Being not amenable to complete unification. We find what Husserl called regional ontologies. We do not find a single, unified idea of Being. In his major work, *Being and Time*, Heidegger orients us towards the idea that the Being of our being is time, and he arrives at this conclusion by bringing to light the idea that we essentially are. But can we, from the idea that the Being of our being is time, go on to conclude that Being as a whole is time? To do so, we must first reduce all the other forms of Being to the Being of our own being, for there are besides ourselves such beings as mountains or rivers, such beings as tables or lamps, such beings as mathematical entities, such beings as living creatures. Heidegger does not tell us whether these various beings are reducible to ourselves.

Perhaps he believes that beings of the type of mountains and rivers are initially seen as instruments or obstacles, that is to say are not fundamentally different in type from such beings as tables and lamps. Consequently, we could do away with purely objective being, since it is first seen as an obstacle or an implement and only afterwards as pure objectivity. But there would, nevertheless, remain the question whether other beings are dependent upon ourselves.

And we are thus referred back to a problem that we shall leave aside for the moment—the problem of realism and idealism. A unified ontology would be possible only if Heidegger opted clearly for an idealistic theory, which he does not seem to do, and so we are forced for the time being to state that ontology remains in a state of dispersion, that there are ontologies rather than an ontology; and to say that there are ontologies is in a sense tantamount to stating that there is no ontology, for ontology is truly possible only if there is a single idea of a single Being. Heidegger does not lead us to such an idea, and the same could be said of Jaspers, who replaces ontology by what he calls periechontology (theory of Encompassings), and of Sartre.

It is known that Heidegger's great book, *Being and Time*, has not been completed, and especially that the last section of the first part is missing. The reason for this is that Heidegger had thought it possible to solve what he considers the sole problem of philosophy in terms of the existence of the Being that we are; he believes, in effect, that there is Being only because of existence. But can an ontology be founded on our own mode of Being? This question has not been decided yet, and that is why after *Sein und Zeit* Heidegger has attempted other approaches to the problem. But he himself knows that none will lead him to the solution, that Being is essentially separate from our being, even though Heidegger can declare in a sense that we and all things are 'in the light of Being.'

Since the publication of *Being and Time*, Heidegger has attempted, in a number of essays and particularly in his commentary on Hölderlin, to erect a kind of mythical philosophy, to teach us the way to a communion with the earth and the world. Gradually he has abandoned the problems centring on *Dasein* in favour of problems centring on the notions of Being and truth, these two notions being ultimately defined, in so far as they can be said to be defined, by each other. And today Being, for Heidegger, is the union of Being itself and the understanding of Being—the union of *Sein* conceived as the Parmenidean Being and the Sophoclean *diké* with the understanding, the *noein*, the *techné*. It is the sum total of heaven and earth, of mortals and immortals.

Heidegger's attempt may be viewed as prompted by the will to go beyond ordinary metaphysical considerations which are, he believes, oriented towards particular beings, in order to initiate us into a meditation he calls ontological, and which seeks to lay hold on Being in its essence. But certain features of Heidegger's thought would lead us to doubt the superiority of the ontological over the ontic. For does not human existence, in so far as it is limited by death, characterize the Being of our particular being? Is it not a fact, secondly, that all reflection on Being in its essence depends on the fact that the particular Being that we are can reflect on Being? Thirdly, in a number of passages, it seems that Heideggerian Being reduces itself to the sum total of beings. Thus the prerogative attributed to the ontological is gradually replaced by a priority, and perhaps even a prerogative, attributed to the ontic. But these considerations, we ought to add, become, or at least might become, less valid as Heidegger continues to philosophize. In *Holzwege* the prerogative of the ontic tends to disappear to make way once again for a less interesting and more classical prerogative of the ontological.

But on the other hand, the study of the history of philosophy shows us, according to Heidegger, that Being reveals itself differently at different times. There is a history of the revelations of Being. And this history affords us a configuration of the profound union of Being and time.

Jaspers, too, as we saw, elaborates different kinds of Being—empirical Being, the Being that we are, scientific Being—and they cannot be reduced to unity. Or, to use another Jaspersian classification, there is Being—object, Being for itself, Being-subject, and once again we find a plurality of Beings. For Sartre there is Being-in-itself and Being-for-itself.

Behind the Sartrian in-itself there is no doubt an epistemological motive which seems legitimate enough: knowledge is possible only if there is something that is known, and if that something is independent of knowledge. But is it also legitimate to affirm that that something is absolute plenitude, absolute immobility? Does this not amount to making a reality out of an epistemological postulate? And can we not say that one of the least contestable acquisitions of philosophy is the proposition that reality is movement and temporality through and through?

Hand in hand with the epistomological motive there is, in Sartre, a psychological motive: our mind tends ceaselessly to become petrified, stablilized; Sartre describes this tendency to petrification by the affirmation that the for-itself tends continually to transform itself into in-itself. But this psychological motive does not provide any reasons for asserting the reality of the in-itself any more than the epistemological motive; our psychological tendency does not prove the reality of a thing any more than the epistemological postulate.

Behind the Sartrian duality of the in-itself and the for-itself, we find something rather similar to the Cartesian duality of extension and thought. And yet, if the in-itself can be compared to Cartesian extension, the for-itself cannot be said to correspond to thought as Descartes conceived it; it is rather to thought as construed by Hegel that the for-itself may be compared. In this sense, it could be said that the in-itself and the for-itself have a relation analogous to that which could be envisaged between Cartesian extension and Hegelian thought.

It should also be noted that Sartre's in-itself consists not only of the material world, but also of the past, and on this point we could compare Sartre's conception to Bergson's, since in both the material world and the past are coupled together.

To the ontological problem is connected the problem of nothingness. Is the idea of nothingness a legitimate idea ? It is interesting to note that in modern philosophy two philosophers—Bergson and Heidegger—have adopted two absolutely opposed positions on the problem of nothingness. Bergson, in *Creative Evolution*, tries to show that nothingness is a pseudo-idea. We arrive at the idea of nothingness only by the intermediary of the idea of everything and by the negation of the idea of everything. The idea of nothingness is the idea of everything plus the negation of the idea of everything. It is the product of negation. Heidegger takes the opposite view. For him there can only be negation if underlying all things there is nothingness. It must be noted that Heidegger himself—as we pointed out earlier—believes that nothingness is the absence of all beings, rather than the absence of Being, so that his position is finally not very far from Bergson's. Being is not something that can really be negated. What can be negated are beings. And at the end of the postscript to his essay *What is Metaphysics ?*, Heidegger tells us that nothingness, being the absence of all being, is not different from Being, which is the absence of all being. We arrive, then, at a conception that identifies nothingness and Being, in a manner different from that in which Hegel identified them.

There was an attempt in Heidegger, at least at one phase of his thought, to probe into absolute nothingness—an attempt that had never been made before. But it seems that Heidegger himself has not been able to remain constant to his initial ambition.

The attempt to throw light—a dim enough light, as it happens—on the idea of nothingness has been more interesting and exciting than satisfactory.

In Sartre's philosophy nothingness is presented in a form much nearer to Hegelian negativity than to the absolute nothingness of Heidegger. Sartre endeavours to translate all our activities into negative form. The imagination is the negation of the real that we encounter in perception. Perception, in turn, is the nihilation of myself. And I myself *am* nihilation. What we see here is no longer the metaphysical attempt that we saw in Heidegger, but rather the application of a will to underscore the restrictive and negative aspects of all that is in our mind.

We said a moment ago that the question of the value of ontology in these philosophies is linked to the question of idealism and realism.

Heidegger tries to overcome the alternative between idealism and realism. Bergson and William James had made similar attempts. The question is whether Heidegger's attempt is successful.

No doubt Heidegger puts forth some important arguments to show that we must pass beyond the problem as it is ordinarily stated. He tells us that classical philosophy has over-separated the subject from the object, that the being that we are is by nature in the world, that we must not question the reality of the world, for to do so would be to underestimate our *rapport* with the world. The human condition is precisely such that the reality of the world is not questioned, since we are being-in-the-world. Thus idealism is the product of a separative reflection. Heidegger's views on this point are perfectly legitimate. But what is striking ordinarily, when he develops his ideas to the end, is that he does not manage to remain faithful to his own conception: at times he veers too near to an absolute idealism, at other times too near to an absolute realism, without overcoming these terms, despite all his desire to do so.

Heidegger is very close to an absolute realism when he tells us that man's duty is to let Being be what it is. We must accept Being as it is. And he is also speaking as a realist when he tells us that other beings are independent of the being that we are. If we did not exist, according to Heidegger, other beings would still continue to be, but Being would not, because Being is not independent of our thought of it.

We are here faced with problems extremely difficult to resolve. Heidegger says that beings are dependent upon Being; now, Being is dependent upon our thought of it, and therefore we can conclude that, despite what was just said, other beings are not wholly independent of our thought, since Being to which they owe their being cannot be without our thought of it.

In any case, such are the features of Heidegger's thought that point to realism; but on the other hand, he contends that underlying all things there is freedom. And so behind Heidegger's realism we find idealism—an absolute idealism not unlike that of Fichte. But freedom for Heidegger consists in letting Being be and once again we swing back to realism.

One of the attractions of Heidegger's philosophy comes from the fact that it carries very far the two great tendencies of the human mind: the tendency to insist upon the world of things as almost impervious to the mind and the tendency, so recurrent in German philosophy, to explain everything in terms of freedom. Thus, Heidegger will say, on the one hand, that truth consists in letting Being be, that truth is in beings, and on the other hand, that the source of truth lies in our freedom. But it seems that our freedom, in turn, must be defined as the capacity to surrender to things, so that what we have is a kind of game permitting us to see the face of the universe either in an idealistic context or in a realistic one, and referring us continually from one context to the other.

The Sartrian distinction between the in-itself and the for-itself leads us likewise to ask the question, which is the more fundamental form of Being? Is the for-itself the elemental form of Being? Indeed, the in-itself is said to exist only for a for-itself. But, on the other hand, the for-itself is said to be a kind of absence, a kind of gap in the in-itself. Thus, according to whether the one or the other is affirmed as prior, we are left either with a realism or with an idealism.

In Sartre's thought, then, we find ambiguities rather similar to those found in Heidegger. By his insistence upon the intentionality of consciousness, by his definition of knowledge as a 'not-being', by his conception of a massive in-itself to which consciousness is opposed as a nothingness, by his affirmation of radical contingency, even at times by his insistence upon failure of communion in love, Sartre's philosophy seems to sum up the grounds for the modern world's often justified resentments against idealism. But, on the other hand, the importance accorded to freedom, the influence of such thinkers as Lagneau and Alain, point in this same philosophy to an idealism. Perhaps the duality that we have found in Heidegger as well as in Sartre is a characteristic, and not the least valuable, of these philosophies; perhaps they reveal themselves thereby as the embodiments of what has sometimes been called the problematism, the ambiguity of contemporary thought.

As regards the concept of freedom, we find a problem similar to that of idealism, the questions of idealism and freedom being evidently rigorously linked to one another.

It was seen that these philosophies, which appear to be philosophies of freedom, are at the same time philosophies which endanger the idea of freedom, philosophies in which freedom appears to be dominated or submerged by its negation—dominated by transcendence and grace in the philosophies of Kierkegaard and Jaspers, submerged by necessity in the philosophy of Heidegger. And in Sartre's philosophy our acts can be interpreted in terms of our freedom, but Sartre would not deny that, in a certain way, they can also be interpreted in terms of our situation.

We are here faced—as we said—with questions very close to idealism and realism, particularly as regards the question whether in Sartre's philosophy there is a unique act of freedom, a unique project that forms us—something analogous to the timeless act by which, in Kant, the individual chooses his character—or whether there are constant possibilities of change in our freedom. There is here an antinomy in Sartre's philosophy, since to be, for the for-itself, is to be what it is not and not to be what it is; to be is therefore to be constantly able to negate one's past acts, for not to negate them would be letting them sink back into the in-itself. But, on the other hand, if I am a person there must be an overall project to characterize my being as a whole. There is thus a struggle between the idea of unity and the idea of multiplicity, both being in a sense essential to the definition of our freedom.

From the idea of freedom we can go on to that of communication and the problem it presents in the philosophies of existence. We have already seen the difficulties of interpretation that this question involves in Sartre's philosophy. According to some of his interpreters, what was said in *Being and Nothingness* applies only to the unauthentic. At the time of writing *Being and Nothingness*, it seems, Sartre believed that there was an impossibility of communication in love relationships, but we must take into account both the diversity of interpretations and the evolution of Sartre's thought, which has on this point gone beyond his position in *Being and Nothingness*. And perhaps it is true that in that book he was referring to unauthentic love only.

We must also take care to distinguish between the different interpretations that Sartre gives of love; besides a need for self-justification, love is, on the one hand, a desire to possess another's freedom, failing by its very nature since one cannot possess another's freedom, and on the other hand, a desire on the part of the for-itself to freeze itself into a kind of in-itself.

What has been said explains the pessimistic aspect that Sartre seems to have given, at least in *Being and Nothingness*, to his philosophy. But perhaps it is not so pessimistic as it appears at first sight, and perhaps Sartre has left behind this aspect of his thought. The fact remains that the formulas which have enjoyed the greatest circulation are formulas such as: 'Man is a futile passion', or 'Man is condemned to be free', or again 'Hell is others', that is to say three formulas emphasizing failure—and we have said that these philosophies are, generally speaking, philosophies of failure.

The question may be asked whether human relationships are marked by hostility as Sartre claims. In *Being and Nothingness* the existence of others is often looked upon by him as a menace. Does not this view of Sartre fail to take into account all the forms of human relationship and perhaps itself call for an existential psychoanalysis?

It could be said, moreover, that Sartre has outgrown the narrower features of his philosophy as presented in *Being and Nothingness*. Today he admits the possibility of free relationships between people, as he admits the reality of social action. On this point as on certain others, the works of Merleau-Ponty show in what direction the ideas of Sartre could be completed; and generally speaking, the philosophy of Merleau-Ponty, by its emphasis of a return towards the immediate, by its admission of communication, by its recognition of the fecund character of ambiguity characteristic of the human condition, paves the way for new developments in existentialism.

The Ultimate Problems of the Philosophies

Let us go back from Sartre to the Heidegger of *Sein und Zeit*.

Heidegger enumerates three aspects of existence: the project oriented towards the future; its determination and conditioning by the past; and thirdly, the essential character of man which is that of a fallen being. But does not the affirmation of this last aspect, which strikes us immediately as different in its structure from the other two, imply a certain conception of man that cannot be maintained if the overall conception of Heidegger's philosophy is to be maintained? Does not the notion of man as situated in a kind of dereliction, of abandonment, imply a number of presuppositions that have not hitherto been accorded a place in Heidegger's philosophy? Man cannot feel abandoned unless he feels abandoned by someone—by God. Thus we find ourselves in the strange position where, if we carry Heidegger's thought to its logical conclusion, we are led to destroy some of the most basic feelings that characterize Heidegger's thought in *Sein und Zeit*. It has even been suggested that Heidegger frequents the world of Nietzsche with the feelings of Kierkegaard and the world of Kierkegaard with the feelings of Nietzsche. This was the case at least until *Holzwege*.

Thus the third aspect of existence implies a pessimism which is open to question. But even the second aspect, the determination by the past, is perhaps tinged illogically, or if not illogically at least unnecessarily, by the sombre nuances of pessimism.

But these tendencies were to be corrected by the considerations of *Holzwege* and even more so by those of a very short piece, *Feldweg*, which, like the commentaries on Hölderlin, opens the way to hope.

Questions may also be raised as to the rôle of the feeling of dread in Heidegger as well as the rôle of nausea in Lévinas and Sartre. Ought these feelings, along with that of boredom to which Heidegger resorts at times, to enjoy such a special status in the philosophies of existence?

For Heidegger, orientation towards death is an essential part of the definition of existence. But one may well ask if the objections of Sartre are not valid on this point and if death has not been given undue importance.

This consideration leads us to a further consideration concerning the essence of time. If time is essentially directed towards the future, our individual existential time will be ended, overwhelmed by death. But to the philosophies that take the future as the basic dimension of time, that is to say the philosophies of Hegel, certain neo-Kantians, and Heidegger, one could oppose the philosophies of Husserl and Sartre, who say that it is in terms of the present that time must be defined.

What has been said allows us to understand the generally pessimistic mood that has been associated with the philosophies of existence. It is certain that the importance accorded by Heidegger to the ideas of care, abandonment, death, the rôle of the idea of failure in Jaspers, some of Sartre's formulas which proved the most popular at first, continue to give an impression of pessimism. It is not quite clear to what extent this impression is due, on the part of the reader, and even perhaps on the part of the authors, to a certain nostalgia for religion.

It was moreover seen that Jaspers, by means of the ideas of the instant and transcendence, Sartre, by the development of his social thought, surmount or try to surmount this pessimistic phase.

Kierkegaard reproached Hegelian philosophy for lacking a conclusion, meaning by this that it did not yield a moral. We may ask what moral conclusion could be drawn from the philosophy of existence. The doctrines of Jaspers and Heidegger appear to be locked up in a kind of moral formalism. Jaspers tells us that the existent is characterized by choice; and no doubt in his own action, Jaspers, when Germany was under Nazi rule, adhered to certain principles with a courage worthy of respect. But for the reader who has only studied his great book, *Philosophie*, what appears is a multiplicity of possible choices, each capable of being existentially lived, and none—at least among the authentic ones—receiving preference. Defiance and confidence, respect for the 'Law of Daytime' and the 'Passions of Night' are all possible attitudes among which we may legitimately choose. The one thing that man must ultimately do is to accept himself as he is. And it is to a similar conclusion that we come in the philosophy of Heidegger. Generally speaking, the philosophies of existence can only urge man to accomplish what Kierkegaard called repetition, to effect what Heidegger calls the act of resolute decision. The nature of this resolute decision itself is left undetermined, though it is said to consist in the recognition of the fact that life is by its very essence terminated.

It has been remarked that, in the moral sphere, the philosophies of existence result in a kind of formalism and that they tend to encourage one or the other of two extreme attitudes: a quietism which would accept everything or an activism whose action would be without foundation. 'It is difficult,' writes Helmut Kuhn, 'to maintain that Heidegger's adherence to Nazism in 1933 was a logical consequence of his philosophy. Only the illogicality of this step was logical. The mechanism of freedom, anguish and fear may catapult the individual to almost any position offered by the circumstances.' What existential ethics demands of us is to decide to decide. But, as the same author points out, 'a philosophy of resoluteness is under suspicion of being an irresolute philosophy.' 'The thesis of total freedom excludes commitment to any particular cause while enjoining commitment to commitments,' and it is certain that the Kierkegaardian idea of repetition, the Jaspersian idea of a large gamut of possible choices and alternatives among which the individual must choose one, the Heideggerian notion of the resolute decision, the Sartrian notion of an infinite and un-varying freedom, plunge us into a quandary whence we can extricate ourselves only by means of certain criteria not given in existential philosophy itself.

Sartre believes that it is always a mistake to raise a particular moment of the past or of the future to a privileged position and to judge the whole of one's life in the light of that moment. It is always a mistake to choose either a moment in one's future, for example, a post to which one aspires, or a moment in one's past, for example, a moment of particular excellence, and to entrench oneself definitively within that moment.

But the question may be asked whether it is not, on the con-trary, a human possibility—one of the most legitimate and even, in some cases, the highest—to strive to perpetuate a moment of excellence.

Helmut Kuhn, in his book *Encounter with Nothingness*, remarks that the philosophers of existence overstep the bounds of the philosophy of existence. The philosophies of existence tend, in the end, to turn into something other than themselves, be it the ontology of Heidegger, the humanism of Sartre, the theory of transcendence of Jaspers. Each of these philosophies, says Kuhn, pass in one way or another beyond the limits of the philosophy of existence proper.

'It is one of the characteristics of Existentialism that its adherents are continually on the verge of apostasy.' Like the Sartrian idea of for-itself, Existentialism is never what it is; it tends continually to transform itself into something else, for example, says Kuhn, into the eschatological neo-paganism and the Dionysiac ontology of Heidegger, or into the humanism of Sartre and his reversion to Hegelian negativity, or, with other philosophers, into religion. Each of Kuhn's assertions calls for a separate examination. Heidegger's ontology appears to be the necessary outcome of a philosophy which was primarily concerned with the problem of Being, and which undertook the analysis of existence only as an approach to Being. Sartre's humanism is in his eyes part and parcel of his existentialism. Christianity is for Jaspers but one of the possible forms of transcendental revelation.

Perhaps Kuhn does not pay enough attention to Jaspers' remark that the philosophies of existence must never be regarded as philosophies which reduce everything to existence; perhaps his idea of these philosophies is too rigid and narrow, although he analyses them with acumen.

The question remains whether a philosophy of existence, in the precise sense of the term, is possible. We have already said that Heidegger and Jaspers are to be distinguished from Kierkegaard in that they have sought to develop a philosophy. But have they not, by developing a philosophy, abandoned something of the character of the subjective thinker as defined by Kierkegaard? In other words, does not the very idea of the philosophy of existence involve an antinomy?

No doubt the existential thinker could reply that he must not let himself be frightened by such antinomies; and this is precisely one of Kierkegaard's teachings. Did not Kierkegaard himself allow the possibility of an existential thought, which is nothing less than an antinomic thought, since Kierkegaard, while proclaiming 'The less I think, the more I am,' admits nevertheless the possibility of a thought in which existence and thought unite and struggle against each other at the same time?

This is a problem that can upset the existentialist's knowledge and even his existence. Does he not, by philosophizing, run the risk of destroying that very existence which he seeks above all to preserve? Perhaps one must choose between existentialism and existence. Such is the dilemma of existentialism.

Everything that we have said shows how difficult it is to make a general assessment of these philosophies, first because of their diversity, and secondly, when dealing with them individually— and this is particularly true of Sartre—because of the diversity of their positions at different periods of their thought.

The Ultimate Problems of the Philosophies

And this leads us back to the assertion that ambiguity is a fundamental category of these philosophies—ambiguity between idealism and realism, ambiguity between freedom and commitment, between pessimism and social action. But this ambiguity is possibly one of the sources of the value and the popularity of these philosophies, for it characterizes contemporary man, as Alquié has remarked in one of the articles he has devoted to Sartre's philosophy, and no doubt even perennial man.

It is thanks to this idea that existentialism can meet some of the objections that we have raised against it. Sartre's thought as expressed in *Nausea* is quite different from his thought as expressed in *The Flies*. We saw likewise a duality between his idealism and his realism, between his ontological tendencies, his phenomenalistic tendencies, his phenomenological tendencies, between the idea of freedom and the idea of commitment, between an intermittent stoicism and a recommendation of action, between pessimism and confidence. But his ambiguity, as we have already said, is characteristic of today's man and perhaps of man of all ages. The impossibility of justification and the search for justification intertwine in Sartre's philosophy. There is, as we said, the Sartre of *Nausea* and there is the Sartre of *The Flies*. There is also the Sartre of *Morts sans Sépulture*, who combines the two contrary tendencies. There may yet be a Sartre who will go beyond ambiguity.

We have alluded to the heterogeneity of the various features that enter into these philosophies. We dwelt upon the ontological feature which ought perhaps not to be so essential to the philosophies of existence. On the other hand, the phenomenological element, to judge by the works of Sartre and Merleau-Ponty, is gaining in importance. Here again we are witnessing a dialectic in the history of this philosophy, which began with the solitary meditations of Kierkegaard and which results finally in a meditation on perception and on union with the world.

The philosophies of existence raise many problems which they do not solve. But what is more important is that we cannot ignore these philosophies.

One of the consequences of the existentialist movement is that we have to destroy most of the ideas of so-called 'philosophical common sense' and of what has often been called 'perennial philosophy'—particularly the ideas of essence and substance. Thanks to this movement, we have become conscious of the necessity of questioning all philosophical concepts and of denying the existence of rational and pre-existent essences.

In the second place, the existential feature proper in these philosophies invites us to a kind of sharpening of subjectivity. This is the Kierkegaardian feature of the philosophy of existence.

In the third place, their phenomenological feature permits us to experience more than ever before our union with the world, to discover that which is prior to reflection and judgement, to arrive at the sphere of the pre-reflective, the pre-predicative, to surmount the dichotomy between idealism and realism.

In this way we become conscious of the movement of transcendence which is present in existence itself. Kierkegaard and Husserl, two of the most important inspirators, and the most unlike, make us understand that we do not exist without something other than ourselves.

To exist or not to exist, that is always the question. And there is always the second question: what does it mean to exist? To exist is to have a *rapport* with the Other (which means God, for Kierkegaard), with others, with the world (to exist is to be outside oneself), and it is also to have a *rapport* with one's own self, to converse with one's own self. Every genuine individual, since the beginning of man, exists. Although to exist is, for Kierkegaard, to be in fear and trembling, for Sartre, to will always and always to fail to achieve one's project, it is nevertheless possible to conceive of an existence where the individual is in a state of joy before all things, in communication with other individuals, and free at last from fear and trembling.

Doubtless we have noticed, in our study of these philosophies, that we find ourselves time and again before impasses. Impasse in Heidegger: we do not know whether it is finally an idealism or a realism that he advocates, though his ambition is to go beyond both; we do not know whether nothingness is or is not identical with Being. Impasse also in Sarte, and return on certain points, perhaps even retreat, from the conceptions of Heidegger towards those of Hegel and Husserl. But the consciousness of such impasses does not mean that we must, or can, turn back; the dogmatisms in whose name the philosophies of existence are attacked render it that much more imperative for us to reaffirm their importance and their rôle. Let us remember that philosophy has quite often found itself in apparent impasses which have later proved to be thoroughfares. Perhaps, in order to facilitate the way out of these difficulties, it would be well to distinguish more and more carefully among the different features that we have enumerated: the insistence upon solitude and the insistence upon communication; the insistence upon freedom and the insistence upon the situation; the insistence upon existence and the insistence upon transcendence. The necessary distinction between different problems, different levels, different features would lead us to see that the problematical character of these philosophies can at least make us conscious of fundamental philosophical questions and of ourselves *qua* questions. In these philosophies, existence and transcendence, solitude and communion, freedom and situation, eternity and history struggle against one another and are nurtured by one another.

A Note on Dread

AMONG the philosophers of dread—or perhaps rather of anxiety—mention must be made of Pascal, if he may be called a philosopher, and of Lequier.

The word dread or anguish (*angoisse*) comes up frequently in Lequier's writings, for example in the passage on '*la feuille de charmille.*' He thinks of himself as a child, aware of the fact that he can set in motion a chain of events: he can break off or not break off the tree branch. 'I can no longer tell between the dreads of the adult that I am and the dreads of the child I was then.' He thinks of the whole of nature as participating in his dread.

In *Abel et Abel*, he describes 'the birth of an anxiety.' 'So it is that standing on the edge of a high cliff, a man is sometimes seized by a feeling of anxiety . . . Drawn inexorably as by the dizzying motion of a whirlpool, he sees himself in the abyss, the abyss engulfs him.' This is the giddiness to which Renouvier, the author's friend, has accorded an important place in his psychological and moral philosophy.

And we might even extend the field of our considerations and speak of dread in the works of writers such as Poe, Kafka, Henri Michaux, Blanchot—or even in Hamlet. But let us limit our subject. As Heidegger has said, 'It was Kierkegaard who made the most thorough study of dread.'

Kierkegaard had read Hamann, who speaks of dread as a 'sacred melancholy,' and describes it as preserving man from total corruption, and sees in it the proof of our heterogeneity in relation to the whole of nature.

He had read Schelling, who insists upon giddiness, the anguish of nature, and even the anguish of God.

But it is not in terms of influences that one can explain the central rôle of dread in Kierkegaard's thought; it is rather in terms of Kierkegaard the man, in terms of his life, dread-ridden from beginning to end. He tells us himself, speaking of the rigorous education his father gave him, that 'this education was to plunge me into sadness and dread.' He speaks of childhood anxieties born of prohibitions imposed upon him by this father: 'If a child was told that it is a sin to break his leg, in what dread would he live, and perhaps he would even break it more often.'

He is familiar with temptation; he experiences the dread that is attendant upon temptation. He seeks, at a certain period in his youth, the truth that resides in evil, and 'the whole of reality,' he writes, 'fills me with dread, from the smallest gnat to the mysteries of Incarnation.'

Dread in the face of sin; dread in the face of the possibility of having a stable family life: he breaks his engagement. Dread in the face of Christianity: 'I suffered such dread in the face of Christianity, and yet I felt drawn towards it.'

Dread plays an essential rôle in Kierkegaard's thought in that it is one of the factors which deliver him from Hegelianism. In a philosophy where Being is said to be plenitude, rational and clear, there is no room for a phenomen such as Kierkegaardian dread which is basically ambiguous, on the one hand, and linked to nothingness, on the other.

We have already alluded, in reference to Kierkegaard's childhood, to the fact that for him dread is born of prohibition: the prohibition imposed by God on Adam was the cause of the first dread. Already in innocence there is a dread, the germ of a dread: latent at first, it is roused by prohibition. What happens then? Man awakens to possibility and is assailed by the dread of possibility.

The two ideas of dread and possibility are intimately linked together. There is in us a knowledge which is not quite aware that it is knowledge, for possibility results from the combination of ignorance and knowledge; it is being and non-being; it is lived as dread.

Now the presence of possibilities, good possibilities and evil possibilities, is the cause, especially in the case of evil possibilities, of temptation, which is a weakening of our will.

Appendix

'There is here a captivating anxiety which fascinates us like the serpent's eye,' says Kierkegaard, 'and plunges us finally into the reality of evil.'

As dread is linked to the idea of possibility, it is also linked to the idea of ambiguity. What we find in dread is a kind of power by which we are attracted and repelled; it is an antipathetic sympathy and a sympathetic antipathy.

What appears here is essentially the idea of ambivalence and at the same time the idea of dialectic. One is drawn towards something which one cannot and does not wish to look at and which at the same time one cannot not look at.

The bond between dread and possibility is further strengthened by the fact that dread is always turned towards the future. One ought to make a study of the relations between dread and time. Dread is always oriented towards something that has not yet occurred. But, at the same time, there is a kind of slowing down of time. When one is in dread, time goes by more slowly, and when one is in the height of dread, time goes by extremely slowly, and one has the sensation of no longer being able to move. And yet, at the same time, it could be said that the instant of dread is a decisive instant. There are therefore, three rather incongruous ways in which dread is related to time: it is oriented towards the future; it slows down the passage of time; and yet it is an instant, a decisive instant.

From the idea of possibility we can also go to the idea of freedom. Dread is the giddiness of freedom. Freedom is caught in its own trap; it is its own captive.

Are we free or are we determined? Or again, are we innocent or are we guilty? We are free and determined, we are innocent and guilty. We are not guilty yet; nevertheless, it could be said that we have already lost our innocence; dread has already taken hold of us, or rather we have given in to dread. Thus we are never sure whether we are free or determined. Man feels guilty without knowing when he has been guilty, for we are not conscious of the moment when we become truly guilty.

Dread produces simultaneous feelings of necessity and freedom, and at the same time we are seized by an anticipatory feeling of repentance as it were, because we already see ourselves as having committed the act that we did not want to commit. And all that remains for us to do, even before the act, is to surrender to remorse.

Dread and possibility; this leads us to another idea which was to be developed by Heidegger: dread is connected to nothingness. There is a positive nothingness, and it is revealed to us in dread. In the philosophies of antiquity, according to Kierkegaard, there was hardly a place for nothingness. With Judaism and Christianity, we come to the idea of a creation *ex nihilo*, to the idea of sin as the manifestation of an active moral nothingness within us, to the reality of time.

One might also mention the bond between dread and what Kierkegaard calls spirit. For man, according to Kierkegaard, is not composed only of soul and body: he is founded on something which ties the soul to the body, and this is spirit; and the more a man is spirit, the more is he in dread. Kierkegaard said of himself: 'Ever since childhood I have been spirit.' But, on the other hand, dread is also linked to the body, and it is the intensity of the consciousness which a man has of being a spirit that leads him to become also conscious of the fact that he is a body. Never was man more conscious of his body as opposed to spirit than since the advent of Christianity. Thus dread is linked both to the presence of the spirit and to that of the body; and the more the spirit is felt as spirit, the more the sensible world will be felt as sensuality.

One could dwell upon the different forms of dread that Kierkegaard distinguishes—dread before sin, dread after sin, but which is really always a dread before sin, for sin is never-ending; dread in paganism, for even in paganism there is an obscure feeling of guilt; dread in Judaism, dread in Christianity, Judaic dread coming from the idea of law, Christian dread, from that of paradox. We shall not insist upon these different elements which have not been retained by Kierkegaard's successors.

What is to be done with dread? In what way can it be of use to us? 'One must,' Kierkegaard tells us, 'school oneself in the most terrible possibilities.' He calls himself, 'the student of possibilities.' 'We must anticipate our destiny by means of dread, and welcome every terrifying experience that comes our way. Dread corrodes everything belonging to the finite world and lays bare all illusions; it extirpates that which is mediocre in us.' Thus, to know oneself to the utmost, one must have experienced dread to the utmost, to the point of death and annihilation. Dread moulds the individual by destroying all his finitudes; it educates him in an infinite manner. And it is in dread that we demand the presence of God.

It is at the moment when we believe ourselves completely lost that aid arrives. Thus dread is the remedy for dread; it purifies the air, renders all things more pleasant finally, more agreeable, more inward, and more surprising at the same time. But dread does not disappear just because we accept this aid; there is a new dread: dread before the Paradox, dread before the Other, the Absolute, which our mind cannot fully grasp, and from which it nevertheless cannot turn away.

All this is but one aspect of a divine action, according to Kierkegaard. It is, as it were, a choice of God which is effected by dread, if we can turn away for a moment from the side of man to catch a glimpse of the side of God.

But dread is always with us: it is inherent to our human condition. Consequently, even in happiness—as we saw in connection with paganism—there is dread. We try to escape from the consciousness of dread by taking refuge in diversions which Pascal spoke of. Nevertheless it abides, since it is the essence of man, in so far as man partakes of the absolute and is drawn to evil, in so far as he is at once a temporal being and an eternal being, in so far as he is a spirit. Man is therefore the more fully man as his dread is the more profound.

Later, after his treatise, *The Concept of Dread,* it seems that Kierkegaard was inclined to give to despair, which he considered more active, more masculine, and at the same time more particular, the importance that until then he had accorded to dread. But whether we call it dread or despair, the two phenomena are very similar.

Thus, dread, according to Kierkegaard, allows us to understand how man has sinned in his freedom, while at the same time allowing us to hold that man is determined. And in everything he wrote about dread, we find what could be called the Kierkegaardian rhythm, that is to say the idea that we must go from one extreme to the other, from the lowest to the highest, from the extremity of dread to the thought of beatitude. We are not to choose the one or the other, but rather to choose the one and, by the one, to choose the other.

By dread, by the crisis of dread, we accentuate our individuality and at the same time, we bring it into contact with the unknown.

What is the rôle of dread in Heidegger's philosophy?

In the first place, Heidegger brings to light more clearly the rôle that dread can play for a philosopher. 'What is needed,' he says, 'is a phenomenon that can unlock Being for us.' There must—and this is a postulate—be something in man that can give him access to the Real itself; and this something is not intelligence; it is feeling, what Heidegger calls *Befindlichkeit*. Fundamentally, every feeling reveals to us something of the essence of things, but there is a special feeling—the feeling of dread.

'Every feeling,' says Heidegger, 'has an intentionality, is directed towards some reality: it is not a fugitive, superficial appearance; it puts us in touch with something.'

Now, on the one hand, dread is a kind of sharpening of our individuality. This idea which was implied in all Kierkegaard's thought is made explicit in Heidegger. Dread individualizes the human being, unifies him in his most original tendencies.

But, on the other hand, it brings us into contact with something; we can hardly say what; something extremely general. Dread is characterized by its indetermination. Fear, fright, are caused by definite things, but dread has a thoroughly indeterminate object. There are no bases from which dread advances upon us; the object of dread is nowhere; we cannot locate that which throws us into dread.

And this brings us to the idea of nothingness. After a paroxysm of dread we tell ourself: actually, there was nothing to be in dread about; I was in dread over nothing at all. According to Heidegger, we are not aware of the truth of our statement; it is exactly the *nothing* that is the cause of our dread.

But behind the idea of *nothing*, Heidegger finds something else. Dread shows us something which is a nothing, because it is not any particular being, to use Heidegger's own language, but the world as a whole.

And that is why dread is a special phenomenon. It reveals to us what Heidegger calls the world, i.e. that which surrounds the individual, that without which the individual cannot exist. It is thus the fundamental feeling, since it is the world as such that it reveals. And our fundamental nature, according to Heidegger, is exactly to be-in-the-world. Dread reveals to us the world as a totality. That which Kant had denied the existence of, and probably rightly, from the point of view of theoretical reason, is grasped from the point of view of feeling, of *Befindlichkeit*, by Heidegger. We have a feeling of the world as a whole. That is why dread is a phenomenon of special status, a *Grundbefindlichkeit*.

The rôle of dread in Heidegger is essentially to allow us to distinguish between the authentic and the unauthentic. Heidegger, in effect, begins with the observation of the everyday world, that is, of the world as it is discovered by pragmatists, of the world of objects and obstacles. But this first consideration of the world must be destroyed so that we may turn our attention to a world of profounder reality, and this can be done only by means of the phenomenon of dread.

In Heidegger, as in Kierkegaard, dread is essential to man; although it appears rarely, it is a constant phenomenon. Its very rarity is proof that we flee from it through dread of dread.

It is consequently not surprising that few philosophers have analysed the phenomenon. 'One could,' he says, 'cite Saint Augustin, and Luther, but not so much for phenomena of dread as for phenomena of fear.' Kierkegaard alone, according to Heidegger, has made a true study of dread.

But we must triumph over dread. And we can do so only after experiencing it in our innermost being, by meditating on death, on the impossibility of possibility, which is at the same time the possibility of impossibility. It is by way of dread of death that we can approach the highest state of authenticity. That dread is our reaction to death is proved by our very flight and cowardice before dread. But it cannot be said that Heidegger and Kierkegaard wish to leave us in dread; they would have us try finally to triumph over dread and to unite it, as they say, with a kind of serenity.

As for Jaspers, he distinguishes two kinds of dread; a vital dread and an existential dread. Vital dread concerns our life and existential dread concerns our existence, the value of our being.

Existential dread occurs in what Jaspers calls boundary situations. In such situations all that is non-essential disappears; and in this sense dread is a kind of metaphysical instrument, or a path towards metaphysics. The giddiness of dread is the deep origin of the philosopher's act, because everything that is pure *Dasein*, in the Jaspersian sense of the word, is wiped away by dread.

But Jaspers, too, tells us that man must triumph over dread, and he must have the courage, in a world without guarantees, to live on and by the values that he creates for himself.

In Sartre, as in Heidegger and even in Kierkegaard to a lesser extent, dread is linked to nothingness. In *La mort dans l'âme* we read: 'Dread went round in a circle among the flowers and vegetables; it could alight nowhere.' This is the same idea of nowhere that we encountered in the preceding philosophers.

Again as in the preceding philosophers, dread is linked to

freedom: dread, which is the consciousness of freedom, is grasped by freedom.

In Sartre it is particularly linked to the idea that we choose our values without any objective guarantee, that we choose them absolutely by ourselves. 'I find myself in a state of total freedom,' says Sartre, 'and I give a meaning to the world,' as the Nietzschean superman gives it a meaning. I am the foundation of all values— and he quotes the example given by Kierkegaard: if Abraham hears the voice of God and obeys Him, it is in the last analysis because he himself has decided that it *is* the voice of God. Sartre says: 'I shall never find any objective proof, any external sign, to convince myself of it; even if I believe that it is God I obey, I myself am the one who decides that it was the voice of God I heard.' The final decision is our own.

Moreover, we do not make decisions simply for ourselves, but for mankind as a whole. Each of our acts is valid in our mind for the whole of humanity. We are a legislator who, while choosing himself, chooses all men. Sartre's thought here is not very far from Kant's.

It is the synthesis of these two ideas—total absence of objective justification and responsibility for all men—that is the source of Sartrian dread.

Thus, these different philosophers do not account for dread in exactly the same way, but the diversity of accounts shows all the more clearly the necessity of dread in the philosophies of existence. The substantiations are different, but dread is always there in all of them. In Kierkegaard, it is theologically motivated: it allows us to understand man's sin. In Heidegger, it plays a rôle in the structure of his system: it allows us to advance from the everyday world to a world of authenticity.

Are these philosophers justified in giving dread a special status? Does dread deserve such a status? Does not the importance accorded to dread stem from memories of earlier metaphysics?

BIBLIOGRAPHY

On the philosophies of Existence in general: JEAN WAHL, *A Short History of Existentialism*, New York, 1949 (especially for the remarks of Berdiaeff and Gabriel Marcel).— E. MOUNIER, *Introduction aux Existentialismes*, Paris, 1947.— H. KUHN, *Encounter with Nothingness*, Hinsdale, 1949.— H. MOUGIN, *La Sainte Famille existentialiste*, Paris, 1947.— L. PAREYSON, *Studi nel l'esistenzialismo*, Florence, 1947; *Esistenza e persona*, Turin, 1950.—P. PRINI, *Esistenzialismo, Studium*, Rome, 1953.

On Kierkegaard: Jean WAHL, *Etudes Kierkegaardiennes*, Paris, 1951.

On Jaspers: Jean WAHL, *La pensée et l'existence*, Paris, Flammarion, 1952.—Jeanne HERSCH, *L'illusion de la philosophie*, Paris, Alcan, 1936.—M. DUFRENNE et P. RICOEUR, *Karl Jaspers et la philosophie de l'existence*, Paris, Ed. du Seuil, 1947 (cf. J. WAHL, 'K. Jaspers en France', *Critique*, t. IV, June 1948).

On Heidegger: P. CHIODI, *L'esistenzialismo di Heidegger*, Turin, 1947; *L'ultimo Heidegger*, Turin, 1952.—A. DE WAELHENS, *La philosophie de Heidegger*, Paris 1945.—Max MULLER, *Existenzphilosophie im Geistigen Leben der Gegenwart*, Heidelbert, 1949.—E. LEVINES, *De l'existence à l'existant*, Paris, 1952.

On Gabriel Marcel: P. RICOEUR, *G. Marcel et K. Jaspers*, Paris, Ed. du Seuil, 1948.—E. GILSON et divers, *Existentialisme chrétien, G. Marcel*, Paris, Plon, 1948.—P. PRINI, *G. Marcel e la metodologia dell'inverifiabile*, Rome, Studium 1950.— P. TROISFONTAINES, *G. Marcel*, Paris, Vrin, 1953, 2 vol.

On Sartre: CAMPBELL, J.-P. *Sartre ou une littérature philosophique*, Paris, 1947.—G. VARET, *L'ontologie de Sartre*. Paris, 1948.— JEANSON, *Le prolème moral et la pensée de Sartre*, Paris, 1947.

Index

Index

Index

Heidegger, 3 n., 11, 25, 103, 106,
108; adherence to Nazism, 105;
and communication, 79–80; and
Dasein, 22, 42–3; and dread,
67–8, 103, 111, 114–18; and
facticity, 7, 54, 61; and finitude,
69–70; and freedom, 61, 63–4;
and guilt, 69; and limitation,
69–70; and meaning of
existence, 36–8; and Sartre, 24;
and school of Husserl, 9, 22,
85; and time, 42, 51–2, 54, 104;
authenticity and unauthenticity,
72–3; *Befindlichkeit* and *Grundbefindlichkeit*, 116; concept of
care, 41–2; concept of world,
36–7; critique of sciences, 18;
differences from Kierkegaard,
21–3; different forms of being,
42–8; evolution of system,
20–1; *existentalia*, 93; *Geschichtlichkeit*, 21–2, 51; *Geworfenheit*,
54; idealism and realism,
99–101; idea of God, 23; idea
of nothingness, 69–72, 98–9;
idea of repetition, 74–5; idea of
resolute decision, 64, 104, 105;
idea of the instant, 56; influence
of Eckhart, 71; influence of
Kant, 11; influence of
Nietzsche, 8; on Being, 10,
38–45, 91 n., 92, 95–100; on
essence, 4–5, 12–13, 37–8; on
metaphysics, 70, 98; on source,
53; ontology, 41, 105–6; on
transcendence, 46; on truth
and Being, 85–6; orientation
towards death, 103–4; *Seinsverständnis*, 40–1; *Vorhanden*
and *Zuhanden*, 42–3
Heraclitus, 44
Holzwege (Heidegger), 23, 41, 43,
45, 64, 97, 103
Husserl, 18, 24, 37, 46, 51 n., 104,

108; and phenomenology, 9,
85, 95; influence on Heidegger,
22, 85; school of, 9–10

Idealism, 96, 99–101, 107
Ideas, theory of, 12–13; the Idea
as totality, 15
Instant, idea of, 56, 59, 104

Jacobi, 8
James, William, vii, 99
Jaspers, 3 n., 5, 24–5, 50, 55, 56,
62, 67, 101, 106; and Cartesianism, 53; and choice, 58–9, 104,
105; and *Dasein*, 35 n., 39–40,
42, 51, 117; and communication, 21–2, 79, 80; and dread,
67, 117; and existence, 30–1,
34, 52; and freedom, 60–6; and
guilt, 69; and Hegelianism, 17;
and repetition, 63, 74–5; and
the Unique, 77; and tran-
scendence, 35, 45–9, 91 n.,
104–6; critique of science,
17–18; differences from
Kierkegaard, 21–3; evolution
of system, 20–1; exposition of
possible viewpoints, 23;
Geschichtlichkeit, 21–2, 51; idea
of failure, 73–5, 104; idea of
truth, 84–5; influence of Kant,
11; influence of Kierkegaard,
10, 77; influence of Nietzsche,
8, 10, 48, 77; influence of
pantheists and mystics, 11;
'Law of Daytime', 58–9, 104;
on Being, 39–40, 44–5, 95, 97;
on boundary situations, 56, 74,
117; on source, 53; 'Passions of
Night', 58–9, 104; periechontology, 96; truth-multiplicity,
83–6
Jeanson, 80
Job, Book of, 8

123

Index